# A SUSSEX GUIDE

# AN
# ECCENTRIC
## TOUR OF SUSSEX

PETER BRIDGEWATER

*Illustrated by*
CURTIS TAPPENDEN

SNAKE RIVER PRESS

# SNAKE RIVER PRESS

**Book No 4**
*Books about Sussex for the enthusiast*

Published in 2015 by
SNAKE RIVER PRESS
South Downs Way, Alfriston, Sussex BN26 5XW
**www.snakeriverpress.co.uk**

ISBN 978-1-906022-03-7

This book was conceived, designed and produced by
SNAKE RIVER PRESS

ART DIRECTOR & PUBLISHER *Peter Bridgewater*
EDITORIAL DIRECTOR *Viv Croot*
EDITOR *Robert Yarham*
PAGE MAKEUP *Richard Constable & Chris Morris*
ILLUSTRATOR *Curtis Tappenden*
CONSULTANT *Lorraine Harrison*

This book is typeset in Perpetua & Gill Sans,
two fonts designed by Eric Gill

Printed and bound in Poland

---

## DEDICATION

*To Gerald Woods (1942-2004):*
*artist, friend, teacher and inspirational eccentric!*

# CONTENTS

# INTRODUCTION

*'Do not fear to be eccentric in opinion,
for every opinion now accepted was once eccentric.'*
BERTRAND RUSSELL

*An Eccentric Tour of Sussex* is a guidebook with a difference. It will take you on an entertaining and sideways journey to some of the more unusual attractions to be found in the county and show you both the eclectic and the surprising. The definition of eccentric is odd in behaviour or appearance, weird, whimsical, slightly quirky or silly and this describes our 20 destinations perfectly. Sussex is sometimes referred to as 'silly Sussex', possibly because the word silly comes from the Saxon *saelig* or *soelig*, meaning blessed or fortunate and Sussex is indeed blessed with more than its fair share of the silly and bizarre.

My choice of venue is selfishly personal. What is extraordinary to one person is commonplace to another but my rationale for inclusion is that each place we visit must be accessible to the public, there must be something enjoyable and interesting to see when we get there, and it must be slightly bonkers. If, like me, you have a dread of dull trips to dreary places that take themselves too seriously and a pathological fear of the mundane excursion with its gaggle of sleepwalking tourists, I guarantee you'll find something here to amuse and entertain.

I first came to live in Sussex in the early 1970s, when I was an art student studying graphic design at Brighton Art College. I well remember being utterly gobsmacked at my first sighting of the astonishing Royal Pavilion (*see p.28*) situated just across the road from where I was to spend three years learning about printmaking, typography and books. I could just glimpse the Pavilion's bizarre onion-shaped domes and flamboyant architecture from my studio window (wonderfully lit at night in those days by ever-changing psychedelic coloured lights). My feeling of disbelief and amazement, combined with euphoria at being away from home, whetted my appetite for the unusual venue, and I have been an enthusiastic fan ever since.

The Pavilion is a loud and radical statement created by a prince with the money and hedonistic self-confidence to realise it. Fashions change and so do our views on the acceptable face of art. The great thing about creativity is that it's driven by self-expression, which we are all capable of, whatever our status.

> *The Pavilion*
> *Cost a million*
> *As monument to Art*
> *And the wits here*
> *Say it sits here*
> *Like an oriental tart*

This song from Noel Coward's *Conversation Piece* (*1934*) sums up what many critics really thought of this eccentric masterpiece. Social climate and popular culture play their part but art dictates fashion and true eccentrics don't care about popular trends or what others think.

Many people consider eccentrics as mad or weird but they are simply unusual and different from the crowd and they sometimes do extraordinary things. John Fuller was nicknamed 'Mad' Jack because of his penchant for building follies (*see p. 24*). His pyramid-shaped tomb in Brightling is bizarre by conventional standards and his neighbours must have thought he had lost the plot when he started building. But his ornamental 'follies' (buildings with no apparent function that aren't quite what they seem) now enrich the landscape and add colour to our world.

Whoever said 'the best thing about Peacehaven is the road out' was misinformed. Peacehaven was once raw farmland, developed in the 1920s by one man into what he was convinced would become a seaside paradise. Those art deco aspirations can still be found if you look hard. Peacehaven was not only to be a dream seaside resort, it also happens to be on the Meridian Line, precisely 5586 miles (8993 kilometres) away from Rangoon in Burma (not a lot of people know that) and there is a neglected monument on the cliff tops at Peacehaven celebrating this fact (*see p. 78*).

To natives who have known it all their lives, Brighton Pavilion is in no way extraordinary, it is the everyday. But in no way could it ever be described as ordinary; it is a bizarre and wonderful gem. I hope this tour stimulates and refreshes the senses of everybody, including the most culturally toughened cynics, and revives the ability to enjoy the silliness that lurks all around. *An Eccentric Tour of Sussex* isn't a guidebook for the seriously minded or the cultural snob; it's entertainment and fun aimed at the connoisseur of the peculiar – one who appreciates the whimsical, is open minded and prepared take an unconventional look at their surroundings. This is culture but maybe not quite as we know it!

I've tried to be even-handed in my choice and geographic spread of venues but inevitably the coastal resorts are centres of eccentric excellence. There are simply more attractions to be enjoyed on the south coast than anywhere else. Every part of Britain is splendid to those who love and appreciate it but we in Sussex are particularly lucky – stunning coastlines, bohemian towns, weird characters (historical and contemporary), fabulous art and a rich cultural history. Sussex has it all and we should cherish and enjoy it.

This tour guide aims to entertain you with wacky churches, bizarre tombs, whimsical buildings, quirky houses, unusual festivals and weird characters. As well as showcasing 20 classic eccentric venues, I also list a few other eccentricities nearby – other delights to amuse you if have the time and the inclination. The richness of Sussex is inexhaustible and there are many curiosities not included here. I don't pretend to know every weird and eccentric haunt in the county and I don't claim to be an expert on any of them. I've written this book from the perspective of someone who is interested in their surroundings, has a low boredom threshold, struggles hard against the herd mentality and prefers to visit places not overrun with visitors (almost impossible).

It is said that the true adventurer is happier to travel than to arrive but few of us are intrepid enough to follow that particular path. In truth, most of us prefer the well-trodden one. We like to aim for something, be guided there safely (stopping for tea and cake on the way), then enjoy ourselves on arrival. Unfortunately, getting there is sometimes a hassle. Most sensible people realise that we can't keep using our cars for every journey because the roads (let alone the planet) cannot sustain the traffic.

The trouble is the car is so damned convenient! However, do brave public transport whenever you can – it can be challenging for the heart and mind. There are drawbacks but the railways still offer a good alternative (as long as the toilets are working) and on a good day, the trains really can take the strain. As two of my eccentric rendezvous celebrate the great age of Victorian railway travel (*see pp.16 and 82*), it seems appropriate to enhance and celebrate the experience by using locomotives for the journey. Go on, it might be fun!

I tackle the practical problems of how to get to my weird and wonderful destinations only briefly (I do expect you all to have a map and some initiative) in my 'Getting there' bit. Although one or two of my inclusions are slightly off the beaten track, most are easy to find. I supply brief instructions for travelling to all 20 main venues plus Ordinance Survey Map reference numbers for cartographical purists.

We're nearly ready to set off, but before we go, I leave you with this amusing quip to take with you on your journey:

*The English like eccentrics. They just don't like them living next door.*

JULIAN CLARY

Finally, sightseers, they say that travel broadens the mind, but you must have the mind to broaden and the desire to broaden it! In my quest I haven't explored every corner of Sussex, I haven't even tried. You may well know better and even stranger places to visit than those included, so if you do, let me know.

I've tried to be accurate with all my information but if you spot any errors or would like to contribute ideas for future Snake River publications, please get in touch via our website: *www.snakeriverpress.co.uk*. In the meantime, gird your loins and come with me on *An Eccentric Tour of Sussex*.

PETER BRIDGEWATER

# ECCENTRIC
# DELIGHTS

# CAMELOT ON THE DOWNS

## ARUNDEL

### Where is it?

Arundel is 90 minutes away from London by train, standing between the Sussex Downs and the sea in the middle of stunning countryside, officially designated as outstanding. It is off the main A27 about halfway between Worthing and Chichester, inland from the coastal resorts of Littlehampton and Bognor (you won't be able to miss the castellated skyline). Straddling the River Arun and boasting a boatyard, pleasure boats, a classic Georgian high street, quaint little side streets and fine town houses, plus a cathedral and magnificent castle, Arundel fully justifies the guidebook cliché of picturesque.

### What is it?

A gobsmackingly large and fairytale-style castle that totally dominates the town and which could easily be the film set for a Hollywood medieval costume drama of *Camelot* or *Ivanhoe*. Arundel Castle, built on the site of an earlier Saxon fortification, totally commands the landscape and is one of the most complete and impressive castles in Britain. With its massive scale, striking appearance, theatrical battlements and towers it embodies every schoolchild's image of what a castle should look like. Everyone who lives in Arundel must feel reassuringly safe. The fortification's lofty location on a hill at the top of the town makes it appear completely protective and in charge of the town and all of its surroundings. The first sight of Arundel Castle must have made potential invaders quake in their boots and turn tail at the prospect of trying to breach it – it looks unassailable. If you haven't seen it before then the best way to enjoy the castle's magnificence for the first time is to drive into Arundel from the east, towards Chichester. As you come over the brow of a hill the castle sits before you in all its dominant splendour. It looks fantastic and if I was a foreign invader, with agitated hordes looking for a fight, I'd creep on past!

## What else should I know?

Arundel Castle has the distinction of being both an ancient castle and a stately home and has been home to the Dukes of Norfolk and their ancestors for over 850 years. Its roots go back to Edward the Confessor and William the Conqueror but, as we have limited space, I'll be brief.

Roger de Montgomery, Earl of Arundel, one of William's best mates at the Battle of Hastings, founded it on Christmas Day 1067. He built a stone castle with a motte (central mound) on the site of an earlier wooden one, taking full advantage of this natural defensive site overlooking the South Downs and the Arun across the coastal plain to the sea. Roger was given a third of Sussex in return for building the castle and protecting the approaches to Sussex from enemies. Although a powerful player in the France-versus-England political power game, Roger was mortal like the rest of us and died in 1094 (although it is said that his ghost still walks the castle walls, presumably checking for maintenance). Subsequent battles were waged, deals were done and thus the castle's historic and colourful journey down through the ages began.

Apart from the occasional reversion to the crown, when lines failed, Arundel Castle is now one of the longest inhabited country houses in England. It passed from the d'Albinis to the Fitzalans in the 13th century and then to the Howards of Norfolk in the 16th.

The Howards were at the forefront of English history from the Wars of the Roses (*1455-85*) through the Tudor period to the Civil War, when General Waller seized Arundel Castle for Cromwell's Parliamentarians in 1643. The defences were destroyed and it remained in ruins until

Thomas Howard, the 8th Duke of Norfolk, started rebuilding in the early 18th century. Charles, the 11th Duke known as the 'Drunken Duke' and crony of the Prince Regent, continued these restorations with exuberant enthusiasm in the 19th century.

In 1846, the 27-year-old Queen Victoria and her Prince Albert came over from Osborne House on the Isle of Wight and stayed at Arundel Castle for a few days. There was a major makeover carried out by the incumbent 13th Duke in order to get the house ready. He spared no expense; he built a new apartment block, furnishing it lavishly with fine furniture and art (including a charming newly commissioned portrait of the young queen by William Fowler) and landscaped the grounds. Victoria had a great time and her suite of rooms remain virtually untouched.

Between the 1870s and 1890s the house was extensively rebuilt by Henry, the 15th Duke and he turned the castle into what we see today, a glorious 'Heinz 57' mixture of Norman, Early English Gothic, Gothic Revival, and Victorian restoration.

**Why visit it?**
Apart from being a fabulously eccentric-looking castle that conjures up romanticised Pre-Raphaelite images of King Arthur, Sir Lancelot and the sexy Guinevere, Arundel is stuffed with other treasures, including the prayer book and gold-and-enamel bead rosary that Mary, Queen of Scots, took with her to her execution.

A jewel not to be missed is the Fitzalan Chapel, the burial site of all the Dukes of Norfolk. Built in 1380, it is named for Richard Fitzalan, who was given the castle when the d'Albinis ran out of male heirs. The Catholic chapel is attached to the Anglican church of St Nicholas, which has a separate entrance in London Road. A glass wall and iron grille divides the chapel from the church to show that it is a separate establishment. This arrangement has been in place since 1879, when the Lord Chief Justice of England ruled that the chapel was not part of the Protestant church. Don't miss the twin effigies of the seventh Duke – one showing what he looked like when he died, the other reinforcing the message that we are all dust by showing his body in decay.

There is an equally impressive and over-the-top Gothic style cathedral to the west, opposite the castle – the cathedral of Our Lady and St Philip Howard. In 1868, 40 years after the foundation of Roman Catholic parishes became legal again, Henry Howard, the 15th Duke, commissioned architect Joseph Hansom (*1803-82*, the man who invented the hansom cab) to design a prominent church that could hold its own against the castle and add yet more weight to Arundel's prestigious skyline.

## Other eccentricities

### CLAPHAM WOOD

For anyone interested in black magic, the spooky paranormal or UFOs, I suggest you don your ram's head and visit the quiet village of Clapham. The wood is said to be haunted (weird night-lights and disappearing vicars). Reputedly cursed in 1288 when a local villain announced:

> *I call upon he who knows to damn this accursed village and all its meagre holdings. May the priesthood of this false God soon come to know their fate.*

It has become famous for its oppressive atmosphere, satanic mists, and strange forces affecting drivers' steering wheels, so beware!

### CLIMPING

A nice, rather quirky shingle beach, going west from Arundel on the coast. A great place for a walk or picnic. And just before you get there is Baliffscourt (now an upmarket hotel), an extraordinary medieval fantasy hamlet, built in 1927 by Lord Moyne of the Guinness family as a retreat for his medieval-architecture-loving wife. The diarist Chips Channon, one of the Guinness set, described the interior perfectly:

> *Every guest room resembles the cell of a rather pansy monk.*

**Getting there**　　　　　　　　　　　　　　National grid ref. TQ020074

- Car: off the main A27 Worthing/Chichester coast road.
- Train: National rail services from London/Victoria, Brighton and Chichester.
- Bus: National Express from Victoria coach station, frequent local services.
- Useful website: **www.arundelcastle.org**

# OUSE VALLEY VIADUCT

## BALCOMBE

**Where is it?**

Bestriding the Ouse Valley just outside Balcombe village, between Borde Hill, Haywards Heath Golf Club and Ardingly reservoir. It is best approached by taking the minor Haywards Heath road south out of the village for about 3 kilometres, when the viaduct can be seen on the right as you sweep down into the vale. Get up close by following a marked footpath at the roadside, which gives access into the field where some of the magnificent semicircular redbrick arches stand.

**What is it?**

The Balcombe Viaduct is an eye-boggling marvel of the Victorian Railway Age, built with total confidence by a country at the height of its economic power and dominance.

The birth of the railways opened up the entire country and allowed ordinary people to travel almost anywhere in the land within a single day. The railways speeded up travel and contracted distance; they distributed produce more efficiently, boosted industrial and agricultural growth, enabled coastal and inland towns to flourish and changed the landscape of Britain forever. Sussex was suddenly brought closer to London but to lay the network of lines and accomplish their vision, skilled engineers first had the task of conquering the geography of the land. Armies of labourers had to clear terrain, dig cuttings, construct embankments, blast out tunnels and build bridges. And one of the most spectacular bridges built anywhere in the country is Balcombe Viaduct, a fantastic achievement and a lasting legacy from the Victorians and their fabulous railway architecture. The fact that the viaduct still carries the Brighton to London line with effortless nonchalance shows just how well it was built.

## Who built it?

Queen Victoria (*1819-1901*) came to the throne in 1837 at the age of 18 and ruled for almost 64 years, the longest reign in British history. This period is associated with Britain's great age of industrial and economic expansion and when Victoria died, it was said that Britain had an empire on which the sun never set. And of all the endeavours that the Victorians embarked upon, the railways were one of their greatest. Within 50 years, between 1825 and 1875, the rail network spread throughout the country like a spider's web, as rival investors built competing lines.

Brighton's fortunes first changed in the early 18th century when the Prince Regent went down there to bathe and have fun and games with Mrs Fitzherbert in his exuberant Palace (*see p.28*). By the 1830s it had become the busiest seaside resort in Britain, with over 2,000 visitors a week enjoying its sleazy amusements. After the runaway success of the Liverpool & Manchester Railway, Brighton became the obvious next stop for steam travel and profit-hungry speculators. Constructing railways was a risky and costly business and it took 10 years of arguing over different proposals and surveying alternative routes before the London & Brighton Railways Company (an amalgamation of contending investors) was finally established and given permission to begin their epic undertaking.

The London to Brighton line was finally given the green light by Parliament in 1837, when railway mania in Britain was at its height. The plan was to connect 41 miles (66 kilometres) of new track from an existing London to Croydon line and take the train down to the coast. The task was monumental and the journey took the company four years to complete. It was full steam ahead for the London & Brighton Railways Company; at its peak, it employed a tough workforce of over 5,000 men armed only with brute force, shovels, picks, wheelbarrows, horses and dynamite. It is now impossible to imagine how remorselessly gruelling and dangerous the work must have been but during those four years this army of navvies sculpted the landscape, laid track, blasted out five tunnels (totalling over 3 miles, 5 kilometres), built 99 bridges and created two amazing viaducts – the Preston Viaduct in Brighton (now mostly obscured by office blocks) and our masterpiece at Balcombe. Phew!

The architect for the viaduct and all the stations along the line, including Brighton, was David Mocatta (*1806-82*), supervised by company engineer, John Rastrick (*1780-1856*). The viaduct runs straight, is 450 metres long, nearly 30 metres high, has 37 tall, elegant semi-circular arches (each spanning 9 metres), gracefully tapering piers, stone balustrading and two decorative Italianate pavilions crowning both ends. It is a listed building (recently restored) and remains virtually unchanged since its construction between 1839-41. It is simply a marvel.

The London to Brighton railway reached its seaside destination in 1841, with the first steam train puffing into Brighton Station on September 21 (fastest journey time of one and three-quarter hours).

**Why visit it?**
The Ouse Valley Viaduct is one of the wonders of Sussex. It is a daring, elegant and inspirational engineering achievement and an important example of Victorian railway architecture. However, travelling across the bridge by train gives little insight into the fabulous architectural accomplishment beneath. The views from the window as you rattle across the valley at Balcombe are glorious (I always want to stop the train and get off) but the views from underneath the edifice are staggering. The sight of the viaduct's 37 graceful red-brick arches, rising upwards and stretching across the lush fields of the Ouse Valley make you feel happy. The scene has a mysterious feel-good factor; spirits are lifted and you feel better for being here. This spot is hypnotic and when you're below, gazing upwards, this supernatural sight is overwhelming.

The Ouse Valley is wonderful anyway but the viaduct, confidently snaking its way across the landscape, compliments and enhances the picture.

It is an example of human endeavour improving the landscape. The bridge fulfils its function perfectly but it is built with more grandeur, grace and architectural flourishes than it needs to have and it is impossible to describe in any way that does it justice. You have to go and see Balcombe Viaduct for yourself to appreciate the dynamic and eccentric lengths that Victorian entrepreneurs were prepared to go to in order to fulfil their unstoppable aspirations. Within 50 years, Victorian ingenuity had changed people's perception of distance and spread a network of lines flamboyantly across the country, indeed the world. Nothing stood in the railway's way. Determined and skilled engineers met every challenge with daring imagination and the Ouse Valley Viaduct, with its reflections of classical Roman aqueducts, is one of their great achievements.

## Other eccentricities

### LINDFIELD

A genuinely pretty village with over three dozen architecturally fine houses (suspiciously immaculate) lining one street. It must constitute some sort of preservation record. Pevsner described Lindfield as having 'the finest village street in East Sussex'. The wide tree-lined High Street is a graceful curved gradient with a pond at its foot and a church at the top. Bordering the pond is a memorable and eclectic array of houses and by the church is an even more remarkable group, including Church Cottage (15th century) and Old Place (late 16th century). The Victorian stained glass artist, Charles Eames Kempe lived in the latter and although not all authentic, the combination of three gables, bargeboards, timber framing and brick nogging is magical just the same.

---

**Getting there**                                    National grid ref. TQ311292

❯ Car: off the B2036, midway between Haywards Heath and Crawley.

❯ Train: National rail services from London/Victoria and Brighton, 2-mile (3-kilometre) walk.

❯ Bus: local services to Balcombe.

❯ Useful website: **www.spartacus.schoolnet.co.uk/RAbrighton.htm**

# BLOOMSBURY WORSHIP

### BERWICK

## Where is it?

St Michael and All Angels church in Berwick village is at the end of a small lane, just off the main A27, before the Alfriston roundabout, about halfway between Lewes and Eastbourne as you drive eastwards. The present church was built in the 12th century on older foundations, probably pre-Christian. It sits on a small hill and backs onto open farmland at the foot of the northern edge of the South Downs. Although only a small church, and well hidden in a copse, its shingle spire rises up above the trees, creating a charming picture-postcard landmark.

## What is it?

From the exterior, this ancient building is no more than a traditional Sussex stone-and-flint church; pretty and in a lovely location but nothing spectacular or uniquely interesting architecturally. What places this high up on the eccentric scale is the series of painted murals inside and the choice of painters. These are 20th-century works painted during the Second World War (*1939-45*). The vivid pictures depict the life of Christ against the background of war-torn Britain and are a reminder of what would have surrounded a largely illiterate medieval congregation – bright images designed for their moral edification. The paradox here is that both artists were bohemian radicals and conscientious objectors living in a libertine household just down the road; not exactly the first choice for a conservatively minded and patriotic community at the height of the war! There were many objections from the congregation at what was considered a scandalous decision by the local bishop in choosing unpatriotic 'free thinkers' to decorate their church and at the 'fleshy', rather than spiritual, images that they created. However, the murals were made and despite church politics, were greeted with great enthusiasm when they were finally installed and dedicated in October 1943.

Influenced by the grand frescoes of Renaissance Italy, this fascinating series of painted murals is a unique example of Bloomsbury art and as such, is unmissably eccentric. The fact that they were painted at all is quite amazing. St. Michael and All Angels church is a modest little country church and an unlikely setting for radical art. The paintings adorn the whole church and were painted onto panels in a neighbouring barn at Charleston, rather than directly onto the walls. The artists posed for each other in biblical costumes as well as using local farm workers and their own children as models and you can see the influence of 1940s hair-styles in the painting of the angels' hair.

## Who made it?

The idea of decorating the church came from the Bishop of Chichester, George Bell, and the murals were painted by two members of the Bloomsbury Group: Duncan Grant and Vanessa Bell (no relation), with the help of her children, Quentin and Angelica. Grant was recommended to Bishop Bell by his friend, Sir Charles Reilly, professor of Architecture at Liverpool University, who knew Grant's aunt, Violet. At the time Duncan Grant was living with Vanessa Bell at nearby Charleston, an old rented farmhouse on the Firle estate, just outside Lewes. Grant was experienced in producing murals and the Bishop wanted to encourage artistic patronage and form closer links between the church and the arts, as well as revive the long tradition of wall painting in Sussex churches.

The Bloomsbury Group was a loose association of artists, writers and creative intellectuals, formed in the first half of the 20th century.

The group stemmed from student friendships made at Cambridge and included E.M. Forster (writer), John Maynard Keynes (economist), Virginia Woolf (writer), Vanessa Bell (artist), Lytton Strachey (writer), Roger Fry (artist and critic), Duncan Grant (artist) and Clive Bell (art critic). They never referred to themselves as 'The Bloomsbury Group' but because they met regularly in the Bloomsbury area of London for their discussions and debates, the association with the name Bloomsbury stuck. This non-conformist group eventually became as well known for their tangled personal relationships and sexual freedom as for the innovative influence that they had on 20th-century culture.

Vanessa Bell (*1879-1961*) was the elder sister of Virginia Woolf and a central figure in the group. Although married to Clive Bell, the great love of her life was Duncan Grant, who was bisexual and had previously been involved with Vanessa's brother, Adrian. Vanessa had three children, Julian and Quentin Bell, and Angelica, her daughter by Duncan. In 1916 the two artists set up house together at Charleston. It became their home for the next 45 years as well as the country venue for the Bloomsbury Group and a mecca for artistic and cultural life. The house and gardens became the couple's creative canvas and they decorated the interiors and furniture from top to bottom with their flamboyant work.

Bell and Grant continued living together harmoniously at Charleston, in an open relationship, until her death and he remained there until shortly before his own death in 1978. The house is now owned by a charitable trust, originally set up by Quentin Bell to preserve the house and work and for the benefit of the paying public.

**Why visit it?**

Like them or loathe them, the paintings have put Berwick church firmly on the Bloomsbury map, along with Charleston, where the two artists lived and Monks House in nearby Rodmell, where Vanessa's sister Virginia Woolf (*1882-1941*) lived with her husband Leonard. The Bloomsbury Group is now inextricably linked to this part of Sussex and these three venues have all become a shrine for Bloomsbury groupies and an important part of our cultural history.

The writer and journalist Cyril Connolly (*1903-74*) is buried at Berwick. Connolly was editor of *Horizon*, an influential literary magazine, between 1939 and 1950, and gave a platform to a wide range of both distinguished and emerging writers. His best work was as an astute critic and his views informed the thinking and attitudes of his generation.

## Other eccentricities

### FIRLE CHURCH

For graveyard connoisseurs, Vanessa Bell, Duncan Grant and Quentin Bell are all buried in Firle church, just a few miles from Berwick. There are also two lovely stained glass windows by the artist John Piper (*1903-92*), showing the sun and moon.

If your ideal recipe for a good day out is famous graves, visit Folkington Church, just up the road, where you will find Elizabeth David's, Britain's most revolutionary cookery writer.

### LITLINGTON TEA GARDENS

Stop for tea and cake in the remains of a lost Victorian Pleasure Garden. During its heyday, in the late 1800s, Victorian holidaymakers would drive out from Eastbourne to stroll through its formal gardens and take tea. Litlington is still a pleasure: excellent refreshments served in romantic garden shacks by nubile girls in starched aprons.

### LULLINGTON CHURCH

Reputedly the smallest in Britain, this pretty flint building overlooking Alfriston is the remains of a larger 12th-century church. Jokingly referred to as the Cathedral on the Downs, it seats 14. The actor and writer Dirk Bogarde (*1921-99*) spent his childhood in Lullington.

**Getting there**  National grid ref. TQ518049
- Car: off the A27, between Polegate and Lewes.
- Train: National rail services from London/Victoria and Eastbourne, 2-mile (3-kilometre) walk from Berwick station.
- Bus: National Express from Victoria coach station, community buses at weekends.
- Useful website: **www.tate.org.uk/archivejourneys/**

# FULLER'S FOLLY

## BRIGHTLING

**Where is it?**

Sitting in the churchyard of St Thomas à Becket in Brightling, a small but picturesque village 9 kilometres north of Battle, first settled after the Norman Conquest. The church itself is 13th century with later additions and, for a country church, larger than one might expect. St Thomas has had many wealthy benefactors, including John 'Mad Jack' Fuller (*1757-1834*), a wealthy 18th-century industrialist, who lived in the nearby manor house on his estate, known as Rose Hill in his time, but now called Brightling Park.

**What is it?**

John Fuller's tomb. Fuller was the extremely wealthy and popular squire of Brightling, who led an illustrious life, pursued a colourful career in politics, never married, became a philanthropist and patron of the arts and sciences and then died at the respectable age of 77. He is buried in the corner of his local churchyard. Looking around peaceful old churchyards is usually a sombre and reflective and sombre pastime: studying ancient headstones, deciphering weatherworn inscriptions, contemplating the universe and trying to grasp the essence of other people's lives. There is no such subtle reticence in the case of John 'Mad Jack' Fuller; he is buried beneath a towering 7.6-metre high stone pyramid that dominates the entire churchyard!

In true Egyptian pharaoh style, Fuller started preparing for his journey into the next world 24 years before the event, constructing his pyramid between 1810 and 1811. Legend insisted that he was entombed dressed in top hat and tails, seated at a table fully laid out with a meal of roast chicken and claret but, unfortunately, this was found to be myth during restoration work carried out in 1982. Fuller is in fact buried conventionally beneath the marble floor. A metal portcullis protects the pyramid's doorway and inscribed on the stone wall opposite is the sobering ninth verse from Thomas Gray's 'Elegy in a Country Churchyard':

> The boast of heraldry, the pomp of pow'r
> And all that beauty, all that wealth e're gave
> Await alike th' inevitable hour
> The paths of glory lead but to the grave.

Fuller's pyramid is a bizarre tomb by any standards, erected by local masons after delicate negotiations with the vicar. These included Fuller gifting the church a new churchyard wall, two substantial stone entrance pillars and an iron gate. This was a man who wished to be remembered and to Fuller size really did matter.

Jack had many friends in the arts, including the famous architect Sir Robert Smirke (1781-1867), best known for his Greek Revivalist public buildings, including The British Museum, Covent Garden Theatre, Somerset House and The Royal Mint. Smirke had travelled extensively both in Italy and Greece and probably helped Fuller draw plans for his exotic and grandiose tomb.

## Who made it?

'Mad' was the nickname applied to Jack because of his penchant for building follies – ornamental buildings which enhance the landscape but aren't quite what they seem. On his 20th birthday, Fuller inherited a very large family fortune and estates. His wealth was founded on iron smelting and the manufacture of iron products, including weapons, but by the time Jack inherited, the foundries in Heathfield (once employing half the local population), had closed. Thus he took possession of land, property, money, investments, an assured future and plenty of time to indulge his fantastic whims.

Jack was a well connected, large, outspoken man, who both enjoyed and fostered his 'eccentric' image. He served as MP for Southampton once and for Lewes twice, as well as being appointed High Sheriff of Sussex. He retired from politics, rather disgraced, after insulting the Speaker of the House of Commons in a drunken debate about the French.

It was after this scandal that Fuller's career as a philanthropist really took off. He commissioned paintings from various artists, among them J.M.W.Turner, funded scientific research, founded two professorships, was a founding member of the Royal Institution, sponsored Michael Faraday's pioneering work into electro-magnetism, endowed Sussex with its first lifeboat, financed the building of the Belle Tout lighthouse at Beachy Head (see p.44), bought and restored Bodiam Castle, and set about building the follies that gave him his name.

## Fuller's other follies

Fuller not only created his own pharaoh's tomb but also several other slightly loony architectural fantasies in the vicinity.

### OBELISK

The Obelisk, or Brightling Needle, was built around 1815, possibly to celebrate Wellington's victory over Napoleon, and serves no other purpose than as a landmark, and statement of Fuller's eccentricity. It is 20 metres high and stands on Brightling Beacon, the second highest point in Sussex at 197 metres above sea level.

### OBSERVATORY

This elegant structure was designed by Sir Robert Smirke as a working observatory, so is only a folly by association and built in 1810, when it was considered fashionable to support astronomy. It is believed that the inspiration for the observatory came from Fuller's friend Sir William Herschel (1738-1822), the king's private astronomer, best known for his discovery of the planet Uranus in 1781. The Observatory is situated on the Brightling–Burwash road and is now a private residence.

### ROTUNDA TEMPLE

Built around 1810, the temple is a circular, domed building on a hill in the middle of Brightling Park. In all, it is about 7.6 metres tall, built on a raised drum with 12 Doric columns supporting a domed roof and surrounding an enclosed circular room. The noted landscape gardener Humphrey Repton (*1752-1818*), who had drawn up extensive 'improvements' for Fuller's estate in 1806, suggested the building of the temple, and although Jack rejected most of Repton's suggestions, he took this one up. There are rumours that Fuller held gambling sessions and wild parties in the Temple and that it was the venue for his romantic liaisons. Brightling Park is now run as a racehorse training school, so the temple is only accessible on event days. Check access dates with Brightling Park on 01424 838241.

### SUGAR LOAF

Built between 1810 and the late 1820s. It is 10.6 metres high and 4.8 metres in diameter and stands at Woods Corner (on the B2096), on the southwest side of Brightling Park. Fuller made a bet while in London that he could see the spire of St Giles Church, Dallington, from his estate. He couldn't, so he quickly built this giant cone to win his wager.

### TOWER

This is a circular two-storey tower with Gothic entrance and battlements, 10.6 metres high and 3.6 metres in diameter, hidden in a small copse opposite Brightling Park. Built while Fuller was restoring Bodiam Castle, it seems likely the castle influenced its design.

---

**Getting there**                                   National grid ref. TQ683210
- Car: off the B2096 and A265, between Battle and Heathfield.
- Train: nearest station Etchingham, 5 miles (8 kilometres) away.
- Bus: local services.

# A PAVILION TOO FAR

## BRIGHTON

**Where is it?**

In the cheeky and celebrated coastal resort of Brighton; famous for its 'kiss-me-quick' tackiness, massage parlours, illicit weekends in seedy hotels, amusement arcades, diverse lifestyles, weird occultists, hard shingle beaches, candy floss, fish and chips, Graham Greene's *Brighton Rock*, Richard Attenborough's *Oh! What a Lovely War*, The Who's *Quadrophenia*, Mods and Rockers, Chris Eubank, political conferences, the IRA bombing of the Grand Hotel and finally, NOT saving the West Pier, once the most splendid example of Victorian marine cast-iron architecture in the country.

The Royal Pavilion sits in its own gardens behind Brighton seafront and the Palace Pier and is only ten minutes walk from the main railway station. It is at the very end of the main London to Brighton road, the A23, just before the road meets the promenade.

**What is it?**

The Pavilion is a fantastic, magical and decadent royal pleasure palace, built to indulge and satisfy the lavish lifestyle of George, Prince of Wales (*1762-1830*), nicknamed 'Prinny'. Over a 35-year period, the Pavilion was transformed from a simple farmhouse, which George first rented as an informal holiday home, into an astonishing Indian-styled Regency palace and bachelor pad. Brighton Pavilion is a fabulous over-the-top stately dream, which George realised, indulged in and lived out for most of his adult life.

## Who made it?

The Prince of Wales first came to Brighton in 1783, at the age of 21, partly on the recommendation of his doctors, who believed that the sea water and country air would be good for his health. The simple fishing town, then called Brighthelmstone, was taken up and gentrified, transformed by aristocratic and moneyed society into the first chic seaside resort – a fashionable town on the social circuit where the in-crowd of the day came to enjoy the seaside and gamble at the races. Modern Brighton is an equally exciting and eclectic place, a town that caters for all tastes, a favourite venue for city dwellers wanting to enjoy the sea air and indulge themselves, and it has George to thank for that.

The original farmhouse with its seaside vista embodied a simple and pastoral idyll with which Prinny quickly became bored. George, a fashionable, fun-loving, rebellious, passionate, unconventional and cultured connoisseur of the arts, decided to enlarge his house into a grand and luxurious palace where he could indulge his appetites to the full, in a more relaxed atmosphere, away from the formalities and constraints of the royal court and his father, George III.

In 1787, George hired the architect Henry Holland (*1745-1806*), to enlarge and transform the original farmhouse into a symmetrical neo-classical Regency composition of columns, bow windows and iron balconies, with interiors decorated in a fanciful Chinese style. Then in 1815, deciding it was time for a makeover, he called in John Nash (*1752-1835*) to remodel Holland's Pavilion into the Indian-styled palace which exists today. Nash had already worked for George on the development of an area in London known then as Marylebone Park (an area stretching from what is now St James's to Regent's Park) and his most famous work includes Trafalgar Square (layout, not buildings), Marble Arch, Carlton House and many of the elegant crescents and town houses around Regent's Park. Nash's iconic buildings have come to define what is now referred to as Regency style.

Nash adopted an oriental style of architecture on the Prince's conversion partly because of its picturesque qualities and romantic associations but also because he could embrace new cast-iron-based technology in its transformation. He enlarged the building and added the frivolous oriental domes and minarets by superimposing a cast-iron framework over Holland's original neo-classical building. The exterior of stucco and Bath stone was completed in 1822.

### What else should I know?
There was another reason for George to visit Brighton, more compelling than his health, or his headlong pursuit of hedonism. He had begun a passionate and secret affair with Maria Fitzherbert, a young widow whose Catholicism made marriage impossible. So they rented separate houses in Brighton to pursue their affair more discreetly. George secretly married her in 1785 (although the union had no legal validity) and later built a connecting tunnel between her house and the Pavilion. National protocol eventually forced George into marrying his cousin, Princess Caroline of Brunswick, but it was a disastrous relationship and, despite earlier startlingly unsuitable liaisons and rumours of illegitimate children, he remained devoted to Mrs Fitzherbert throughout his life.

### Why visit it?
The Royal Pavilion is Brighton's most famous landmark and if you've never seen it before, prepare to be amazed. The fake façade of eastern domes, decorative minarets, carved pillars and intricate Arabian latticework is unique and somehow perfectly suited to the exuberant atmosphere of Brighton. Now tastefully illuminated at night, the Regency palace is both theatrical and extraordinary.

Nothing can quite prepare you for the breathtaking interiors. Inside, the palace is a sumptuous oriental fantasy world, filled with mythical creatures, magnificent decorations, astonishing colours and superb craftsmanship. Adorned with gilded dragons, *trompe l'oeil* paintings, carved palm trees and imitation bamboo detailing, the palace is a unique mix of Eastern exoticism and English eccentricity.

Every room is dramatic and breathtaking but the scale and opulence of the Banqueting Room beggars all belief. The ceiling is an enormous, wonderfully decorated 14-metre-high dome, filled with the gilded and copper foliage of a gigantic plantain tree and a huge carved dragon holding a massive and radiant jewelled and mirrored glass chandelier. It must be one of the most extraordinary ceiling decorations in the whole world. Not bad for a seaside holiday cottage.

## Other eccentricities

### BOOTH MUSEUM OF NATURAL HISTORY

A wonderfully gloomy museum with over half a million specimens stuffed, labelled and preserved for posterity. Exquisite birds and butter-flies, exotic creatures floating in specimen jars, whales and dinosaur bones; a taxidermist's dream!

*Booth Museum: 194 Dyke Road, Brighton, East Sussex BN1 5AA.*

### BRIGHTON MUSEUM / HOVE MUSEUM

Two fantastic places to go for culture, coffee and cake. For some strange reason, neither museum is very busy but both have great collections housed in wonderful buildings with excellent ambience. Enjoy old movies at Hove, including footage of cyclists peddling off Brighton Pier for fun.

*Brighton Museum, Royal Pavilion Gardens, Brighton, East Sussex BN1 1EE.*
*Hove Museum, 19 New Church Road, Hove, East Sussex BN3 4AB.*

### REGENCY NUPTIALS

If you want to solve a problem for Maria or play Prinny & Co. for a day, you can hire the Pavilion for flamboyant weddings and parties. Go to www.brightonmuseums.org.uk. Theatrically OTT, but memorable!

---

**Getting there**                                    National grid ref. TQ313042
- Car: at the end of the A23/M23, on the A259 coast road.
- Train: National rail services from London/Victoria, Brighton and Coastway.
- Bus: National Express from Victoria coach station, frequent local services.
- Useful website: **www.brightonmuseums.org.uk**

# BIG BROTHER

## CHICHESTER

**Where is it?**

Thorney Island is a peninsula (not quite an island) on the south coast, jutting out into Chichester Harbour, virtually on the border of West Sussex and Hampshire. The nearest cities are Chichester and Portsmouth, both 14 kilometres away in opposite directions. Thorney is just below the harbour villages of Emsworth and Prinsted, separated from the mainland by a narrow channel of water called the Great Deep, which cuts across the entrance to the peninsula. To the southwest is Hayling Island and to the southeast is West Wittering. Access on to Thorney Island is limited and by foot only, via a causeway.

**What is it?**

The name means Island of Thorns and evidence suggests that at one time the land had been used as an ancient ritualistic burial ground. The island has been diminishing in size since the 1300s, gradually being taken back by the sea. Thorney Island is mostly off limits to the public because it is an army base and owned by the Military of Defence (MoD). It was a true island in the 19th century but has been joined to the mainland now for over 125 years, ever since tidal mudflats were reclaimed in 1870. It was appropriated first by the Royal Air Force in 1935 and used as a fighter station and base for Coastal Command during the Second World War. In the mid-1970s it became a temporary camp for refugee

Vietnamese boat people and then in 1984 it was taken over by the army. Thorney Island is now the home base for the Royal Artillery Regiment.

The population of Thorney is made up entirely of soldiers and their families. Everyone else needs a security pass from the army to enter but this only allows access onto a curious circular walk around the perimeter footpath. You cannot deviate from the signed path and you cannot get lost. As well as being a secure military base with menacing high fencing, remotely controlled electronic gates and protected access, the island is an important and internationally recognised habitat for wildlife. Thorney Island has become an ornithologist's dream, a walker's paradise and a bizarre location for a Sunday afternoon stroll.

### Why visit it?

Visiting Thorney Island is a must for spy thriller fans and conspiracy theorists. It is a rather surreal 1984 'Big Brother' (in the Orwellian sense) experience. Firstly, visitors have to announce their full names and post-codes to the guardroom at the remotely controlled CCTV security gate, via a press-button microphone. Nobody actually appears but after a short and somewhat insecure delay (what if I'm arrested?), presumably while your identity is checked and okayed by MI5 or some other spooky organisation, you are let through onto the island. You then go through the same intriguing rigmarole when leaving. Access to the footpath is available seven days a week but always monitored.

It takes about four hours to walk the whole route around the shoreline and it doesn't matter which way round you go. The camp's perimeter path takes you along reinforced seawalls, past old RAF hangers damaged by German Luftwaffe air raids, working boatyards, across two lifting bridges and past St Nicholas, a late 12th-century church, with a tie-beam and kingpost roof and Norman windows in the chancel. Although St Nicholas is now standing on the water's edge, when it was first built the island was bigger and the sea much further away. At least you can now look round if it's unlocked. Apart from the church, you have to stay on the path and within the yellow markers at all times. I don't know what happens if you deviate but do let me know when you're released!

At the southernmost tip of the peninsula is Pilsey Island , which can be reached on foot at low tide. Again, you are allowed to walk the shoreline but nowhere else. Although once a bombing range, Pilsey is now a bird sanctuary to be enjoyed only through binoculars. To add to the bizarre 'Cold War' intrigue of this particular eccentric outing, it is worth noting that Pilsey Island made headline news in 1956, when the alleged body of Lionel 'Buster' Crabb, a British Navy frogman and employee of MI6 was found floating off Pilsey Island – minus his head and both hands. Crabb had vanished on April 19th during a reconnaissance mission around the Soviet cruiser *Ordzhonikidze* while it was on a diplomatic visit to Portsmouth Harbour. Although there is much speculation about assassination and double agents, we will all have to wait until 2057 to find out the truth, when official documents regarding Crabb's disappearance are due to be released.

## Other eccentricities

### CHICHESTER CATHEDRAL

A bit of a pilgrimage but good refreshments are priceless. Apart from expanding your mind and worshipping the miracle of beautiful and inspiring 1,000-year-old architecture, you can enjoy tea and cake in ecclesiastical walled gardens.

### COCKING BALLS

Andy Goldsworthy's 14 giant chalk balls in their downland setting just outside the village of Cocking (12 kilometres north of Chichester), are sculpted Land Art, created to make you think about your environment. Surreal and thought-provoking, they look amazing in the snow!

### EMSWORTH

Picturesque fishing village with fine Georgian houses, walled gardens and mill-ponds, positioned on the western edge of Chichester Harbour. Good base for lazy walks. Drivers beware: if you park on the fishing jetty at low tide you may well return to a submerged car. Bosham, a few miles east, is the equally wet scene of Canute's futile attempt to stop the sea. Maybe his chariot was badly parked too!

## GOODWOOD SCULPTURE PARK

Just outside Goodwood Racecourse, near Chichester, you can see 70 specially commissioned, monumental sculptures set into idyllic woodland. Not cheap to see, or buy (all sculptures are for sale), but they make for a quirky and fun day out.

## WEST DEAN

West Dean College and Gardens at the foot of the downs, has a long and distinguished history dating back nearly 400 years. In 1932, Edward James (*1907-84*), art collector, poet and avid supporter of the avant-garde Surrealist movement inherited the estate. He remodelled Monkton, the Lutyens-designed house, and began filling it with Surrealist excess, including a Dali Mae West's Lips sofa. James later founded The Edward James Foundation, a charitable trust dedicated to encouraging music, visual arts and traditional crafts. He also extended the gardens.

The quirky character and atmosphere of the house and grounds remain. Today, West Dean is a unique community of artists and craftspeople working alongside farmers and gardeners, and it offers a wide range of creative courses. The beautifully restored complex of walled kitchen and fruit gardens has become one of the most impressive in the country and is a highlight to any visit. Abundant harvests of fruit and vegetables are celebrated annually with colourful festivals devoted to tasty favourites such as hot chilli peppers, tomatoes and apples.

Edward's grave, a simple inscribed slab of Cumbrian slate sheltering amid exotic trees and Himalayan rhododendrons, lends a suitably melancholic air to this rustic vision.

---

**Getting there**                                        National grid ref. SU755031
- Car: off the A27 between Chichester and Portsmouth.
- Train: nearest station Emsworth, 1-mile (2-kilometre) walk.
- Bus: Regular 'Little Nipper' buses from Emsworth.
- Useful website: **www.defence-estates.mod.uk/access/walks/walks/walks_thorneyisland.htm**

# BOHEMIAN RHAPSODY

## DITCHLING

**Where is it?**

Ditchling is about 13 kilometres inland from Brighton, between Lewes, Hurstpierpoint and Burgess Hill. The quickest and easiest way is to head north out of Brighton on the A23; the far more scenic route is across the South Downs from the A27 out of Brighton and over Ditchling Beacon – scary on the downhill bends but well worth it for the wonderful panoramic views. You can stop off at the beacon to enjoy the view at your leisure.

**What is it?**

It's a small and picturesque village at the foot of the South Downs with the usual mix of narrow higgledy-piggledy streets, pretty church and olde-world teashops – seemingly a village full of charming and respectable antiquity. Who would have thought it the scene of libertine free love, incest and all-round bohemian artistic action?

For Ditchling is now indelibly linked with the artist Eric Gill (*1882-1940*), who founded an influential artistic and religious commune there during the early part of the 20th century. Gill and his wife first came to Ditchling village a year after they were married in 1907 and then settled in a Georgian cottage on Ditchling Common. They were quickly joined by other like-minded disciples, including artist and poet David Jones (*1895-1974*), artist Sir Frank Brangwyn (*1867-1956*), sculptor Joseph

Cribb (*1882-1967*), printer and writer Hilary Pepler (*1878-1951*) and calligrapher Edward Johnston (*1906-2006*).

Gill converted to Catholicism in 1913. His devout Catholic views became central to the group and in 1917 the idea of a religious order of craftsmen and women living a fully integrated artistic life was conceived. In 1921, after World War I, he and others founded the Guild of St Joseph and St Dominic, a bohemian community of work, faith and domestic life inspired by the Arts and Crafts movement and medieval trade guilds. The community had its own workshops and chapel and thrived for 60 years. Its affairs were finally wound up in 1989 and the workshops demolished.

Eric Gill was a deeply religious man who saw art as 'man's act of collaboration with God in creating'. He also wrote 'that it seems best to draw whatever is natural and normal and to trust to the good sense of people to see things in a reasonable manner'. His strong Christian beliefs did not inhibit him from being a sexually driven and highly erotic man and this is reflected in much of his work. For example, during his Ditchling years he made an almost life-size sculpture of his sister Gladys and her husband Ernest Laughton copulating, which he simply called *Fucking*.

To the uptight and repressed Britain of the inter-war years, his work would have seemed shocking and indecent. There is an amusing story about Lord Reith, then Director General of the BBC, asking Gill on at least two occasions to reduce the size of the boy's penis in the sculpture of *Prospero and Ariel* that the artist was carving above Broadcasting House. Gill's interpretation of the natural and the normal with regard to his own sexual behaviour was liberal. He was regularly unfaithful to his wife, he indulged in incestuous relationships with two of his sisters, two of his daughters and bestiality with the family dog.

Eric Gill is without doubt one of the great artists of the 20th century – a prolific wood engraver, a master sculptor and an iconic typographer and lettering artist. Gill's achievements also included many important contributions to the art of book production. This very guidebook is typeset in Gill Sans and Perpetua – two classic fonts designed by Gill in the mid-1920s for the Monotype Corporation and now his enduring legacy to typography. A key element of his artistic community was a private press run by Hilary Pepler. The press, called St Dominic's Press, enabled members to circulate ideas and journals and provided them with a creative outlet.

## Why visit it?

Ditchling may be a quiet village that makes surprisingly little of its distinguished legacy, but is a must for lovers of arts and crafts. The eminent potter Bernard Leach had this to say:

*We thought that the place in England that had the greatest vitality and thought in action and craftsmanship was probably the small village of Ditchling, just north of the Downs near the coast at Brighton.*

Many notable artists and craftsmen and women have lived and worked here, inspired by its peaceful Downland setting and rural way of life. The churchyard itself is a stonemason's testament to some of their artistic lives – a Who's Who of creativity carved out on headstones: Edward Johnston, Joseph Cribb, Dunstan Pruden (*1906-74*). There is also a carved stone sundial in the churchyard by Gill to commemorate the coronation of George V in 1911 and a stained glass window in the church by Charles Knight.

Although the village has a rich artistic past, the present is equally vibrant – not all the eminent artists in Ditchling are dead and buried! Raymond Briggs, the creator of such children's classics as *Fungus the Bogeyman*, *The Snowman* and *Where the Wind Blows* lives and works in the village. So do John Lord (another children's picture book artist) and Anton Pruden, the silversmith grandson of Dunstan.

Ditchling's heritage is recorded in Ditchling Museum, a relatively new establishment founded in 1985 by the Bourne sisters, Hilary and Joanna, in the old Victorian schoolhouse behind St Margaret's church. Hilary Bourne's woven hangings and altar curtains hang in the church. The museum has an unusually rich collection that reflects Ditchling's rural, agricultural past as well as its important connection with the Arts and Crafts commune, the Guild of St Joseph and St Dominic, and Eric Gill and his circle.

## Other eccentricities

### BRIGHTON'S FOUNTAIN

'Fountain' is a worldwide healing project based on the idea that concentration on an agreed focal point (Hara) in one's community for a few minutes every day and sending out unconditional loving thoughts can heal the world. It started in Brighton – at the Victorian fountain in the Old Steine (spookily surrounded by ancient Druid sarsen stones, and apparently on a main ley line) when a group of colourful converts (Fountaineers) got together to stop punch-ups between Mods and Rockers in 1970s Brighton. They gathered at the landmark fountain to focus their energy on civic peace and the name 'Fountain' stuck.

### BRIGHTON SEWERS

Brighton's subterranean sewers are a masterpiece of Victorian engineering; 70 kilometres of tunnels built to drain Brighton's ablutions into the sea. If you're brave, have a strong nose and don't mind getting mucky, you can book tours from May to September on www.southernwater.co.uk.

### JACK AND JILL

These two spectacular landmark windmills on the hill above Clayton can be seen from miles away. Jack, the black one, is brick and was built here in 1896. Jill, the 19th-century white post-mill was dragged over the downs from Brighton, by teams of oxen in the 1850s.

### TWO QUEENS

Just along Underhill Lane in Clayton is a humble but much-visited church with fine medieval wall paintings. In the churchyard is the grave of Sir Norman Hartnell (1901-79), the Queen's favourite dress designer.

---

**Getting there**                                National grid ref. TQ325152

❯ Car: off the A23 between Hurstpierpoint and Haywards Heath, on the B2112 and B2116.

❯ Train: Nearest station Hassocks, then a 3-mile (5-kilometre) walk.

❯ Bus: frequent buses from Brighton and Lewes.

❯ Useful website: **www.ditchlingmuseumartcraft.org.uk**

# DOOMWATCH

### DUNGENESS

**Where is it?**

Not in Sussex, is the answer. Dungeness is just over the border in Kent but ranks so highly on the 'eccentric places you absolutely must see before you die' scale, that I feel justified in including it. Every tour is allowed at least one detour and this is mine. You can see Dungeness quite clearly from Sussex as you approach Romney Marsh; it's about 6 kilometres across the border as the crow flies. The nicest route to take is via the B2075, just outside Rye, which meanders through Camber Sands.

**What is it?**

Dungeness is an extraordinarily surreal and barren coastal landscape with a strangely eerie atmosphere and echoes of another world. It is the headland of a massive shingle beach on Romney Marsh and one of the largest expanses of shingle in the world. It is probably most famous for its two nuclear power stations which dominate the location, the first built in 1965 and the second in 1983.

Dungeness is a remote fishing community, not truly a village, more a scattering of fascinating ramshackle wooden dwellings, clusters of huts and upturned boats spread out across the headland. Situated on the very corner of the sparsely populated, open flatlands of Romney Marsh and cut off from everything else, Dungeness has a unique stark beauty and peaceful solitude.

The area is an important protected nature sanctuary with a remarkable and special variety of birdlife and plants that has become a haven for scientists and wildlife conservationists. The Royal Society for the Protection of Birds runs the Dungeness Nature Reserve (over 1,000 hectares), which is open daily except the two days over the Christmas holiday. There are more than 600 different types of sea kale and other vegetation growing among the pebbles (about one third of all the plants to be found in Britain) and an amazing number of insects – rare moths, butterflies, bees, beetles and spiders – many of which are not found anywhere else.

Dungeness also boasts two lighthouses, the Romney, Hythe & Dymchurch Miniature Railway, the artist Derek Jarman's distinctive house and garden, a traditional fish smokery run from a 270-year-old fisherman's cottage and numerous other curious artistic-looking wooden shacks with driftwood gardens.

**Why should I visit it?**

Dungeness is an eccentric treasure-trove in a remote corner of the Kent coast and not to be missed on any account. It is a beautiful place with a remarkably surreal quality. The enormous nuclear power stations whirr away constantly. Many people believe that they are unsafe and irrevocably damaging to the environment; yet, paradoxically, they have enhanced the very landscape they dominate. These two giant, kinetic installations are thermal power stations, cooled by seawater and generating warm-water outflows. The warm water pumped back into the sea attracts birds and wildlife, which in turn flourish in the warmer microclimate.

Before the September 11 attacks on America in 2001, you could look round the stations on guided tours but unfortunately these were stopped in case Al-Qaeda bought a ticket. The smoking stations with their high-fenced perimeters dwarf the area in a slightly menacing way but add greatly to the surreal ambience.

The Romney, Hythe & Dymchurch Miniature Railway, the world's smallest public railway, is yet another big reason to visit Dungeness. The Light Railway Café at Dungeness station serves up typical fare but you can eat it while gazing across the shingle wasteland to the giant power stations and at the same time watch a tiny, brightly painted passenger steam train chug into the station. This is bizarre fun on a grand scale.

The railway was built in 1928 for millionaire racing driver Captain J.E.P. Howey and all 10 of its original steam locomotives are still in use. They puff away between Hythe and Dungeness, stopping at several other little stations on the way, and apart from transporting local children to and from school, they provide curious adults with a uniquely innocent experience in miniature form.

From the Railway Café you can see both of the Dungeness lighthouses that mark out the end of the peninsula for ships navigating the Dover Straits. The oldest, painted in black and white horizontal bands, was built in 1904 and now stands well above the high water line. This was obscured to mariners when the power stations arrived and so a second lighthouse was built in 1961. This stands further east and rises from a white concrete base. The whole tower is flood-lit at night, which not only helps shipping, but stops migrating birds crashing into it. The old lighthouse is open to the public, but the new one is not.

Do not leave Dungeness without looking at Derek Jarman's inspirational garden. Derek Jarman (1942-94) was an influential British film director, stage designer, artist and writer. He was drawn to Dungeness by its desolate character and used the setting for his film *The Last of England* (1986), an allegory on the social and sexual inequalities in England under Thatcherism. When he was diagnosed HIV positive, Jarman dedicated himself to promoting gay rights and increasing public awareness of AIDS. At the same time he began creating his beloved garden at Prospect Cottage, his distinctive yellow-painted, black-tarred wooden fisherman's cottage. Although a relatively inexperienced gardener, Jarman succeeded in combining local plants, stones, driftwood, fishing tackle and metal into a peaceful, unique and thought-provoking haven.

> *On December 22 1986, finding I was body positive, I set myself a target:*
> *I would disclose my secret and survive Margaret Thatcher. I did. Now I have*
> *set my sights on the millennium and a world where we are all equal.*

## Other eccentricities

### PETT LEVEL

A quiet, old-fashioned seaside village, with massive sea defence walls on which you can enjoy bracing walks and fantastic views. Pett is at one end of a 45-kilometre long Royal Military Canal, built at the beginning of the 17th century to stop Napoleon in his tracks. As Bonaparte had already plundered his way across Europe and Africa, I'm not sure an 18-metre-wide canal would have stopped him!

### RYE

A completely mad place! You can find the bones of a murdering butcher (he butchered Mr Grebel the magistrate in 1743) hung up in the Town Hall. Rye Museum (another gem housed in two separate buildings, run by sweet lady volunteers) has a queer mix of relics, including a miniature model of the entire town made by an eccentric local.

Rye, *aka* Tilling, provides the setting for writer E.F. Benson's (*1867-1940*) series of comic novels about two socially competing ladies, Mapp and Lucia. Benson moved into Henry James's former Georgian manor, Lamb House, shortly after James died. The town and its maze of higgledy-piggledy streets form the geographical backdrop to fictional Tilling and his two main protagonists' social rivalries were based on Benson's personal experiences. 'Friends of Tilling' now hold an annual celebration of the writer and you can wander the maze of lanes around West Street, eccentrically re-enacting Mapp and Lucia's fictional adventures on loony literary tours. Rye is east of Hastings on the A259.

---

**Getting there**                                        National grid ref. TR088168

- ❯ Car: A259 and B2075 then private access road to Dungeness.
- ❯ Train: Romney, Hythe & Dymchurch Miniature Railway from Hythe, Dymchurch, St Mary's Bay, New Romney, Romney Sands and Dungeness.
- ❯ Bus: local sevices from Lydd and Folkestone.
- ❯ Useful website: **www.dungeness.org.uk**

# HEADY MADNESS

## EASTBOURNE

**Where is it?**

On the south coast of England, five kilometres west of Eastbourne. The Sussex Downs begin (or end) at Beachy Head, where the chalk downs meet the sea and on a clear day you get fabulous views. Looking east, you can see the beaches and towns of Eastbourne, Pevensey Bay and Hastings, sometimes even as far as Dungeness in Kent, nearly 65 kilometres away. Looking west you can see as far Selsey Bill near Chichester and, if the weather is right, the faint outline of the Isle of Wight, 113 kilometres away.

**What is it?**

Beachy Head is the highest and most dramatic chalk sea cliff in Britain. It rises 162 metres above sea level and is an exhilarating and panoramic beauty spot surrounded by pounding seas, squawking gulls, wind-deformed trees and yellow gorse, with masses of wild flowers during spring and summer. From Beachy Head, the South Downs run west-wards over undulating and unspoilt countryside towards Birling Gap, the Seven Sisters cliffs and Cuckmere Haven. They eventually end at the cathedral city of Winchester. The cross-country route between Beachy Head and Winchester is called The South Downs Way. This old trail of about 160 kilometres traces the spine of the Downs and has been used for centuries by travellers and traders moving between villages.

## Who made it?

This amazing landscape was crafted by evolution and nature. For most people Beachy Head is a place of escape, relaxation, pleasure and well-being. But there is a darker side. Since the 1600s, it has been a notorious site for suicides. Bizarrely, this wonderful natural beauty-spot exercises a powerful and irresistible draw on the minds of those despairing people who come here from all over the globe to end their lives. Beachy Head has become famous for being the world's number one suicide spot and, sadly, about 20 people kill themselves here every year.[1]

## Why visit it?

Beachy Head is a wild and dramatic natural wonder set amongst some of the finest countryside in Britain. It also has a colourful history. The seas are notoriously dangerous with unpredictable currents and strong winds, and many ships have sunk here. It can be extremely cold and windy so be prepared. It is always spectacular but on a sunny evening looking westwards across the Downs towards Belle Tout lighthouse with the light fading, it is a magical and reflective experience.

## What else?

Folklore has it that some of the shipping disasters were caused deliberately when wreckers lured ships onto the cliffs in order to plunder and strip them of salvage and valuables. In the darkness, sea mists and low visibility of a stormy sea, it would be impossible to discern the coast or judge its distance. It seems that criminals on land using moving lanterns would confuse sailors already in trouble into thinking they were actually the lights of another ship. Believing they were heading for safe water, they would sail towards the lights and tragically towards, not away from, danger.

In 1692 Jonathan Darby, curate of St Michael's Church in Litlington and, later, Rector of Wilmington and Parson of Friston and East Dean, decided that a reliable fixed light was essential in order to warn men at

---

1. *There is a Samaritan telephone box next to the Beachy Head Hotel for anybody suicidal who needs support or wants to talk about his or her despair.*

sea of the hazards and whereabouts of the coast. His pastoral duties included the burial of bodies washed up from wrecks and the number of drowned sailors he attended so distressed him that he decided to act. He excavated 'Parson Darby's Hole' in caves already existing near Belle Tout. He created a chimney that led up from the coast and constructed rooms above it where he set lights on stormy nights. Sometimes he spent whole nights there himself, watching the sea. Many lives were saved and even when ships were wrecked, some sailors were saved by being pulled to safety into Parson Darby's Hole. The parson died of pneumonia in 1726 and is buried in Friston churchyard beneath his epitaph: 'He was a sailors' friend.' The cave became a place of curiosity, almost a pilgrimage for a while after his death, then smugglers took it over.

In the early 19th century, an East Indiaman ran aground off Beachy Head and though its crew were saved, a Royal Navy captain petitioned the government to take action to protect its ships. As a result, a light was set up in a wooden hut on the cliff tops near Beachy Head in 1828. It was given the name Belle Tout, which comes from the Saxon war god 'Bael' and the word 'Tout', which means lookout. In 1831, a more permanent stone tower, built on the same location and financed by John 'Mad Jack' Fuller (*see page 24*), replaced the wooden structure. The lamp was first lit in 1834 and although this gave a stronger light, it was still only visible in fine weather. This original lighthouse fell into disrepair and was finally abandoned in 1899 due to serious cliff erosion.

It was then proposed that a new lighthouse be built at the bottom of the cliffs where its light would be enhanced by the reflections from the surface of the sea. The present tower was funded by the Brethren of Trinity House, a charitable organisation for the welfare of mariners, and required a dam around the work to stop the tide flooding the site and an aerial hoist system to lift materials (including 3,660 tons of Cornish granite) from the cliff top to the beach. There was a stone platform for boats to moor and a tower 36.6 metres high. The light, first powered by paraffin, began operating in October 1902. In 1920 electric cable was laid underground to power the lighthouse and in 1983 the lighthouse was de-manned and the whole operation automated.

## Other eccentricities

### BELLE TOUT

In 1999, in a blaze of national publicity, Belle Tout, still a private house, was jacked off the ground in an amazing engineering feat and moved 17 metres inland on specially made sliding tracks, away from the crumbling cliffs and settled safely onto new foundations.

### BIRLING GAP

An atmospheric, eroding coastal hamlet cut into a narrow cleft in the final ridge of the South Downs, just before they climax at Beachy Head. A few fishermen cottages teeter precariously close to the cliffs. Tearoom aficionados must take in the gloomy Birling Gap Hotel on the cliff edge.

### CUCKMERE HAVEN

Spectacular flood plain where the Cuckmere snakes into the Channel (inspiration for Snake River Press). It is where the South Downs and sea collide in high drama and become the Seven Sisters cliffs (the longest natural exposure of chalk cliffs in Europe). Looking back at the estuary from the A259, the view is gob-smacking.

### LONG MAN OF WILMINGTON

This guardian of the South Downs is a giant over 70 metres tall. Marked out in white on steep downland slopes just outside Alfriston, clasping two poles (possibly a rake and scythe), the figure looks as though he's skiing. Tradition maintains that 19th-century prudes rubbed off his erect penis during restoration work, so maybe he was a fertility symbol after all! Whether Neolithic or 18th century, the mysterious Long Man remains popular with Druids.

**Getting there**　　　　　　　　　　　　　　　National grid ref. TV588955

- Car: off the A259 coast road just outside Eastbourne.
- Train: National rail services from London/Victoria and Coastway, 3-mile (5-kilometre) energetic walk.
- Bus: frequent buses from Eastbourne seafront.
- Useful website: **www.eastbourne.org**

# CULT FICTION

### EAST GRINSTEAD

## Where is it?

East Grinstead is in the northeastern corner of West Sussex, midway between London and Brighton on the Surrey/Sussex/Kent border. A well-heeled commuter town, East Grinstead is only a few minutes away from the M23/M25 motorway link, about 11 kilometres east of Gatwick Airport and Crawley, 19 kilometres west of Tunbridge Wells and very close to the open heathland of the Ashdown Forest.

## What is it?

East Grinstead is something of a mecca for mysterious quasi-religious and evangelical cults. It is surely a more than weird coincidence that so many diverse religions have huddled together in this seemingly bourgeois location. The town has certainly attracted more than its fair share of the curious and the quirky. It may be that it sits on a magical convergence of ley lines or simply that it's a nice place to be. Whatever the explanation, East Grinstead is home to: Scientology; the Mormons (*aka* The Church of Jesus Christ of Latter Day Saints – another American import in the form of Joseph Smith, his many wives and 'Book of Mormon' tablets); Kingdom Faith Church, a charismatic independent church; the UK's Jehovah's Witnesses HQ; Opus Dei; the Rosicrucians; New Life Church; the Full Gospel Church, as well as the more conventional mix of Anglicans, Catholics, Methodists, Baptists etc.

## Which cult?

The most famous cult is undoubtedly Scientology. It was founded by Lafayette Ron Hubbard (*1911-86*), an eccentric and controversial American millionaire and science-fiction writer, with 589 published works to his credit. His fantasy and science-fiction books have such catchy titles as *Battlefield Earth*, *Fear* and *An Alien Affair*, while his non-fiction books have more sombre titles – *Scientology: The Science of Certainty*, *Ceremonies of the Founding Church of Scientology* and *The Original L. Ron Hubbard Executive Directives*. Hubbard lived in East Grinstead between 1959 and 1967, during which time he settled well into the local community and contributed enthusiastically to the town's activities. He was East Grinstead's Road Safety Committee organiser, a Parade Marshall and he sponsored children's cycling competitions.

Hubbard bought Saint Hill on the outskirts of East Grinstead from the Maharajah of Jaipur, one of India's exotic playboy Mughal princes from northern India who sold up when his fortune started dwindling after India gained independence in 1947. Saint Hill Manor is an important Georgian manor house and one of the finest Sussex sandstone buildings in existence. Under Hubbard's stewardship the house was restored to its original state, uncovering oak panelling, decorative fireplaces and intricate plasterwork ceilings. Set in 24 hectares of beautifully landscaped gardens, woodlands and lakes, the estate is now an international centre for The Church of Scientology. Its peaceful gardens are open to the public all year round and are a great setting in which to contemplate the meaning of life, including the doctrines of Scientology, which I'm not even going to try to explain.

A few financial facts for the avaricious and curious: Scientology currently holds assets of over $500 million, including a cruise ship used as a seagoing religious retreat, two publishing houses and a 1,150-hectare Californian ranch used as a school, 45 buildings on 200 hectares in California and the British HQ. In 2006 1,300 new missions were opened around the world, including grandiose new premises in New York and the City of London. The Church of Scientology now claims 10 million members worldwide and has proved a smash hit in Hollywood Babylon with shining stars such as Tom Cruise, Katie Holmes and John Travolta all signed up. Hubbard's teachings include 500,000 pages of writing, 6,500 reels of tape and 42 films kept in impregnable reinforced vaults capable of withstanding earthquakes and nuclear attack (but from whom?).

## Other eccentricities

### EMERSON COLLEGE

Down the road in Forest Row is Emerson College, a pioneering and eccentric adult educational centre founded in 1962 and based on Anthroposophy and the doctrines of Rudolf Steiner (*1861-1925*). Steiner's commonsense principles encourage a balanced nurturing of the spiritual and material world, emphasising personal responsibility and social awareness. May the East Grinstead force be with you!

### GUINEA PIG CLUB

During World War II, plastic surgeon Archibald McIndoe (*1900-60*) pioneered new methods (hence the name Guinea Pigs) of rebuilding the badly burned and mutilated faces of injured aircrew at East Grinstead's Queen Victoria Hospital. McIndoe not only rebuilt his patients' faces, he helped them rebuild their self-confidence after their terrible ordeals. The Guinea Pig Club is a survivors group who meet annually in a local pub called The Guinea Pig, in honour of McIndoe. You can also visit the Hospital's own museum.

### MORMONS

Officially called The Church of Jesus Christ of Latter-day Saints, this evangelical church, founded in America by Joseph Smith in 1830, is one of the fastest growing religions in the world. Mormons believe in God, Jesus Christ, the Holy Ghost, The Bible and The Book of Mormon (an ancient record of an early group of Hebrews that migrated to America). Smith claimed to have been visited by an angel (yeah, yeah) who revealed this ancient record on golden plates, which were then translated.

Prejudice and persecution resulted in Smith being murdered and his followers chased across America's central plains (led by Brigham Young) to Utah and Salt Lake Valley, where they settled. Although polygamy is no longer part of their manifesto, plural marriage (more than one wife, are you mad?) was convenient and encouraged childbirth at a time when men were thin on the ground and the group needed to flourish.

Joseph Smith and all successive Mormon leaders are regarded as prophets (like Moses, Abraham and Muhammad but just coming later). Continuing Godly Revelation through prophets, everlasting family unity, strict uncompromising morality, zero drug-taking, 10% income contributions and zealous missionary work (sharing the message) are all guiding lights. Mormons also believe that by praying for lost souls, they can be redeemed back into Heaven. To this end, TCJCLS has created the largest internet genealogy resource in the world, so that ancestors can be traced, prayed for and saved! The UK's Mormon HQ, the brilliant London Temple, in East Grinstead, is only open to fully paid-up members; the rest have to make do with the grounds.

## STAIRWAY TO HEAVEN

Hammerwood Park (just outside East Grinstead and probably the first house in Britain built in the Greek Revival style), was designed in 1792 by Benjamin Latrobe (*1764-1820*), who was also responsible for the White House and Capitol, Washington D.C. The house was bought by 60s and 70s cult rockers, Led Zeppelin, in 1973 and then ignored for 10 years because they completely forgot they owned it. Capitalising on the spiritual synchronicity that enchants all who enter East Grinstead, 30 years on, 'Stairway to Heaven' is their most memorable song.

---

**Getting there**                                         National grid ref. TQ381359

❯ Car: on the A22 and A264, just off the M23.

❯ Train: National rail services from London/Victoria, 2-mile (3-kilometre) walk.

❯ Bus: National Express from Victoria coach station.

❯ Useful website: **www.scientology.org**

# HEAVEN'S ABOVE

### GORING-BY-SEA

**Where is it?**

Goring-by-Sea is a small seaside village on the south coast between Worthing and Ferring, about 3 kilometres outside Worthing town centre on the A259 heading west. Reputedly one of the sunniest places in southern England, it is famous for its acres of horticultural greenhouses growing commercial bedding plants. Between Goring and Ferring is a peaceful expanse of greenery called Goring Gap, one of the very few places in Sussex where farmland rolls right down to the sea. This wonderful stretch of beach forms a natural barrier against development and holds back the tidal wave of urban sprawl, sometimes referred to as 'Boring Goring'.

There is something slightly quirky and 'Stepford Wives' about this coastal community but people who live here seem to love it. Goring-by-Sea has an old fashioned feel-good factor about it and lulls the visitor into a false sense of belief that life lived here could be savoured like one long, carefree summer holiday.

**What is it?**

A copy of Michelangelo's ceiling in the Sistine Chapel, replicated on a smaller scale in a modern catholic parish church. Michelangelo's gigantic and miraculous masterpiece was painted on the vaulted ceiling in the papal chapel at the Vatican in Rome, between 1508 and 1512. It was commissioned by Pope Julius II and has amazed the world with its super-natural beauty and greatness for 500 years.

Our Sussex reproduction was completed in 1993 as an act of religious devotion carried out over almost six years by an untrained artist. It can be found on the ceiling of The Church of English Martyrs, 37 Compton Avenue, Goring-by-Sea.

Michelangelo's monumental Sistine Chapel fresco (water-based paint applied onto wet plaster so that the colour is absorbed and fixed when the plaster dries) represents the mystery of creation and shows Old Testament prophets predicting the coming of Christ. It took Michelangelo four years of lonely, superhuman physical exertion to complete, lying on scaffolding towers painting while looking upwards, and is an astonishing artistic and intellectual achievement. The copy at Goring-by-Sea is two-thirds the size of Michelangelo's and the colours, although much brighter and more lurid than most printed reproductions of the original, are strikingly similar to the colours now revealed on the cleaned and restored original.

## Who painted it?

The Goring ceiling was painted by parishioner Gary Bevans, a professional sign writer and graphic designer. He has no formal training in painting and started his labour of love in 1987 after going on a parish pilgrimage to Rome to attend the beatification of 85 English martyrs. Gary was so captivated and inspired by the wonder of Michelangelo's work that he returned home with a passionate desire to create a replica of the Sistine Chapel ceiling in his own church. With the agreement and encouragement of his priest and parishioners he painted for five and a half years, mainly in the evenings and at weekends, working in modern, quick-drying acrylic paint.

## Why visit it?

As far as I know, this copy of Michelangelo's ceiling in the Church of English Martyrs at Goring is the only known hand-painted reproduction of the Sistine Chapel ceiling in the world (surprise, surprise). Few people would have the commitment, devotion or ability to undertake such a task. Expect to be gobsmacked in Goring but don't expect Renaissance art. Gary Bevans's version of Michelangelo's ceiling is, after all, an amateur imitation of a miraculous and unique masterpiece by a great master, carried out enthusiastically by an untrained fan. This work should be appreciated for being an amazing personal achievement and an expression of loving eccentricity, as well as enjoyed purely as church decoration.

The use of art in churches as a focus for dedication, contemplation and spirituality is an ongoing artistic and religious tradition, and this replica is part of that tradition. Since the painting was completed, it has attracted international publicity and curiosity for both artist and church and has made the Church of English Martyrs a distinguished and quirky tourist attraction.

## Other eccentricities

### BOGNOR BIRDMAN

Every summer, Bognor Regis, westwards along the coast from Goring, holds an annual world-class spectacle in silliness, the Bognor Birdman competition. Aerodynamically-challenged lunatics from all over the world come to Bognor to out-glide each other in this human-powered flying event. Eccentric superhero contestants in an array of silly outfits launch themselves off the end of Bognor Pier and into the sea. A prize of £25,000 is offered to anyone who can defy gravity the longest and fly past the magic 100-metre mark. The all-time record is still held by David Bradshaw, who flew an impressive 89.2 metres in 1992. Splashdown is best!

### CASTLE GORING

An old historic folly with early connections to Percy Bysshe Shelley, the Romantic poet. Construction began in 1790, and it is 'Heinz 57' architecturally; a sort of Palladian villa meets Arundel Castle. It is now a private language school. You can see it from the A27 and, if you ask nicely, you may be allowed access to the grounds.

## THE MILLER'S TOMB

Just outside Goring in a peaceful spot on Highdown Hill, north of Highdown Gardens, is the tomb of John Oliver, an eccentric 18th-century miller. He had the tomb (now under a tree and protected by railings) built in readiness about 25 years before he died in 1793. His coffin was on casters and he kept it under his bed for nightly vigils. He would also make daily visits to his future grave and meditate. John was buried upside down so that when the Day of Judgement comes and the world turns upside down, he will be the right way up. Highdown Hill (a prehistoric fortified settlement, Saxon cemetery and even older than Cissbury Ring) is also the Midsummer Night haunt of Morris Dancers – so beware the sound of jingling bells.

## SEA VIEW

The only literary connection to Goring that I can turn up is that writer and journalist Richard Jeffries (*1848-87*) spent the last two years of his life here. When Jeffries was alive, before the railways steamed into town in 1906, it was still isolated. Goring only became Goring-by-Sea when the post-railway village boomed and there was concern it might become confused with the better known Goring-on-Thames, Berkshire. Jeffries lived in a blandly named house called Sea View and there is a little plaque there to commemorate that little-known fact!

**Getting there** National grid ref. TQ 104032
- Car: on the A259 coast road between Worthing and Littlehampton.
- Train: National rail services from London/Victoria, Littlehampton and Coastway.
- Bus: frequent services from Worthing and Littlehampton.
- Useful website: **www.goring-by-sea.uk.com/englishmartyrs.htm**

# GOING NATIVE

## HASTINGS

### Where is it?

Hastings is on the A259, the main south coast road, about halfway between Eastbourne and Rye. Coming down from the north, the major route is the A21. It goes all the way from the M25 to Hastings and is a pleasant drive. It passes through the rich leafy suburbs of Tunbridge Wells, making a good contrast to our next destination.

### What is it?

A quaint, slightly tatty and depressed old fishing town, Hastings enjoys an air of tired gentility, a rich history and a thriving community of writers, artists and other bohemians. It's the town where John Logie Baird (*1888-1946*) transmitted his first television image and Robert Tressell (Robert Noonan) wrote about socialism in *The Ragged Trousered Philanthropists* (*1914*). It is a town with strong attitude and home to a long line of committed eccentrics.

Hastings was one of the original Cinque Ports; an ancient confederation of five major sea ports established by Edward the Confessor in the 11th century, to help defend England's shores against continental invaders. Hastings provided provisions, ships and men when the king needed them and in return, received royal privileges and trading concessions. But the Hastings fleet happened to be away fishing when William of Normandy invaded in 1066. With an army of less than 10,000 men, the French conquered and occupied Anglo-Saxon England and the date 1066 became a permanent fixture in every English child's mind.

From the late 18th century onwards, Hastings shared a parallel history with many other south coast towns, when sea bathing and water cures became popular. By 1815 it was a fashionable holiday resort. When the steam railway arrived the service from London took longer than the trip to Brighton and so Hastings' new-found prosperity waned. By the early years of the 20th century Hastings was suffering from economic depression. Unemployment was so severe here in the 1930s that the Fascists thought it would be a good recruiting ground. William Joyce, later Lord Haw-Haw (*1906-46*), and Oswald Mosley (*1896-1980*) both came to political meetings in the town, but thankfully there were enough left-wing anti-fascists to see them off.

## Why visit it?

Apart from the spectacular castle on West Hill, the Smugglers Caves (now an 'Experience'), the twisty little streets of Old Town and the extraordinary tall wooden black-tarred fishing huts on the beach, Hastings is well worth a visit for its intriguing occupants.

One of its more unusual citizens is Archibald Stansfield Belaney, *aka* Archie Belaney, *aka* Grey Owl. He was born in Hastings in 1888, emigrated to Canada when he was 17 and adopted an Indian identity. He learned the Ojibway language, became a trapper and hunter, and traded in beaver skins. In 1910 he met and married Angele Eguana, and they had a daughter, Agnes. Archie reinvented himself as Grey Owl, 'noble savage', mixed race son of a Scottish father and Apache mother, adopted by the Ojibway tribe. This was the fantasist biography that Archie presented for the rest of his life. The fledgling Grey Owl was to became a progressive, albeit rather eccentric, conservationist who dedicated his life to travelling the world writing and talking passionately about the environment and his adopted country.

As a rather solitary, emotionally damaged child in Hastings (the son of a drunken father and very young mother, unable to cope), Archie spent most of his time playing in the hills around the town and keeping an unusual menagerie of frogs, mice, snakes and other creatures in the attic of the house where he lived with his grandmother and two maiden aunts, Carrie and Ada. He sometimes took his little friends to school in his pockets and became obsessed with Native American culture and playing 'Red Indians' in St Helen's Wood. It was the hills around Hastings that first inspired his great love of the outdoors.

In Canada in 1925, after his first marriage had failed, Grey Owl met Gertrude Bernard (Anahareo), an Iroquois woman almost 20 years younger than him, who became his muse and encouraged him in his writing about the wilderness. The couple had adopted a pair of beaver kittens orphaned after their mother and siblings had been killed in one of Archie's traps. Gradually, Archie came to appreciate the beauty and intelligence of beavers, already threatened with extinction. His attitude towards hunting changed and he began writing and speaking about the need for environmental protection and awareness. When his first talk to a ladies' club in Ontario raised $700, Grey Owl realised that he could earn a living doing what he loved. His appearance by now was that of a proud, fierce-looking, brown-skinned, inscrutable-faced Native American Ojibway, dressed in traditional fringed buckskin clothes and greeting people with the Ojibway salute – a raised right hand.

Grey Owl became an influential popular speaker and even performed for George VI and Queen Mary at Buckingham Palace. People responded positively to his ecological message. The Canadian Government was persuaded to set up two National Parks and provide secure habitats for his beloved beavers. He was a natural storyteller and his gripping tales were of adventures with bears and lynxes, narrow escapes from death, snow blindness, hardships and other triumphs of survival in the harsh Canadian wilderness.

Archie visited Hastings twice on promotional lecture tours as Grey Owl, first appearing to a packed house at the White Rock Pavilion in 1935. The audience included his aunts who must have been bemused by his Native American incarnation, but discreetly kept quiet. It was only after his second trip to Hastings in 1937, that under pressure from the local press, his aunts admitted to the *Hastings Observer* that Grey Owl was actually their nephew. Grey Owl returned to Canada exhausted by his tour and died the following year of pneumonia. With his death and the ensuing publicity came public realisation that he was not a real Indian. Unfortunately, and unfairly, his conservationist message was assumed to be just as phoney as his identity. With the passing years, however, Grey Owl has been recognised as an important and inspirational environmentalist ahead of his time, albeit a bit of an eccentric showman.

Hastings Museum and Art Gallery in the Old Town has an impressive Native American collection and a permanent display on Grey Owl, including costumes and models from Richard Attenborough's film *Grey Owl* (*1999*) starring Pierce Brosnan.

## Other eccentricities

### DE LA WARR PAVILION, BEXHILL

The UK's first public Modernist dream by the seaside. Commissioned by the ninth Earl De La Warr, the socialist mayor of Bexhill, it was designed by Eric Mendelsohn and Serge Chermayeff in 1935, built of steel and concrete and represented a brave new regenerated world for Bexhill. Unfortunately both it and the town fell into disrepair. What is odd about the De La Warr is that it got built here in the first place. Newly restored as a contemporary arts centre, it's a wonderful, uplifting building.

### HASTINGS JACK-IN-THE-GREEN

Pagan May Day celebrations (in fact a whole weekend of them) with lots of dressing up, 'bogies' with painted green faces, music, drumming and Morris dancers strutting their stuff around maypoles. Colourful, exciting (probably sexually repressed) and undeniably weird!

---

**Getting there**                                      National grid ref. TQ824094
- ❯ Car: at the end of the A21, on the A259 coast road.
- ❯ Train: National rail services from London/Victoria, Eastbourne and Coastway.
- ❯ Bus: national Express from Victoria coach station.
- ❯ Useful website: **www.1066.net/greyowl/**

# THE BLACK PRINCESS

### HORSHAM

**Where is it?**

In the peaceful churchyard of St Mary the Virgin, a pretty medieval brown sandstone building in the centre of Horsham, West Sussex. Horsham is an historic market town off the A24, about 32 kilometres from Worthing and about 13 kilometres from Gatwick and the M23/M25 motorway link. St Mary's stands at one end of an oasis of calm called The Causeway – an ancient area of Horsham blocked off and hidden from traffic between the back of the 19th-century town hall and the church. This attractive building acts as a sort of town and country gate – walk through the churchyard and across the River Arun and you're immediately in open countryside.

**What is it?**

The gravestone of an exotic 18th-century Indian princess, nick-named 'The Black Princess', who was abandoned by her western husband in England and spent the next 50 years of her life living quietly outside Horsham in the heart of St Leonard's Forest.

Immediately on your right as you walk through The Causeway entrance into the quiet churchyard of St Mary's is a long, flat unimposing grey tombstone marked with a large cross and a faded inscription. What marks this out from all the other graves as being slightly odd is that the stone rests on a brick plinth, has no headstone and is oriented north-south instead of east-west. All the other surrounding graves are at a completely different angle.

This is the grave of Mrs Helena Bennett, an eastern princess originally named Halima, who died on December 27, 1853 and was buried on January 4, 1854. What is bizarre for its day is that she was allowed to be buried as a Catholic convert in a Protestant churchyard, lying on her side with her head to the north and her face turned towards Mecca, in accordance with Muslim traditions.

### What else?

Halima or Sakina (*1772-1853*) was an exotic and mysterious woman who ended her days stranded in a foreign country as an eccentric recluse. She was born into a high-class Muslim family in Lucknow, one of the most sophisticated cities in India at the time, the daughter of a Persian Cavalry officer. She may have even been a child-bride to the Nawab of Pundri because in later life she claimed to have once been a 'queen' in her own country.

At the age of 15, in 1788, Halima married a French mercenary soldier and trader, Benoit Leborgne, who was working for the Maharaja Scindia of Gwalior. Benoit, the son of a furrier from Chambery, in Savoie (Savoy), was older by 22 years and would have ostensibly converted to a Muslim in order to marry her. Halima's sister Fraiz also married a British soldier, indicating that inter-racial marriage between westerners and local women was fairly common.

Benoit (by now a general and a successful businessman but in poor health) and Halima had two children: a daughter Buvnoo, born in 1789 and a son Ali Baksh, born in 1792. They seemed happy and in 1796, having become extremely rich (amassing £225,000, a fortune by today's standards), the couple retired to England. The Napoleonic Wars were raging across Europe so England probably seemed a safer bet than France. Calling himself by the more aristocratic name of Benoit de Boigne, Benoit became a British subject and the family moved to Great Portland Street, London. The de Boignes settled into society life. Halima adopted the anglicised name of Helena, after Benoit's mother, and the surname

Bennett. They must have appeared a very romantic and exotic couple to London society at the end of the 18th century.

No doubt Halima struggled hard to adapt to a strange life in an alien environment but this became impossible when her husband met, courted and married Adèle d'Osmond, the beautiful blonde 17-year-old daughter of an impoverished French aristocrat. He became instantly besotted by Adèle and no doubt neglected to tell her about his Muslim family! It was easy to divorce under Muslim law and, anyway, his marriage to Halima wouldn't have been recognised by the Catholic church. In 1798, a few weeks after meeting Adele, they were married and Helena was dumped. As it turned out, the marriage was a complete disaster and they separated after only a year. De Boigne went back to Chambery, Adèle went to Paris and Helena retreated to St Leonard's Forest.

Helena/Halima, still in her early 20s, would probably have accepted her husband taking a second wife because it was allowed under Muslim law but it would have been almost unbearable for her to cope with being abandoned in a strange country with two small children. Everything would have been foreign to her and, as a divorced woman, she was considered a social outcast.

Benoit was rich and took care of Helena financially (appointing a trustee called John Walker to administer her affairs) but we know from letters in the de Boigne archive that she struggled, and the letters have a tragic undercurrent of loneliness. Halima lived reclusively in a small cottage with nearly 200 hectares of land and a maid called Caroline Colin. We know from documents that Helena was a deeply depressed woman, a melancholic who mostly didn't care about her appearance and outlived both her children.

Sometimes Helena would dress up in her Sunday best, wearing flamboyant jewellery and drive into town for the weekend in a pony cart to celebrate mass. It is said that she smoked an oriental hookah pipe, spent money recklessly, was fond of animals and generous to the poor – a harmless but tragic and reclusive eccentric, abandoned in a foreign country.

## Why visit?

If the poignancy of the Princess's grave isn't enough, the town museum alone is worth a visit. The Causeway is a wide tree-lined street (almost like a rectangular town square), bordered by a perfect array of classic text-book houses. These range from an ancient manor to a model group of early 19th-century cottages. Causeway House, now Horsham Museum, is a wonderful 15th-century house with later additions and is not to be missed. Fantastic artefacts professionally displayed in a fabulous building staffed by helpful curators, with a remarkable walled garden at the back. This peaceful space, lovingly tended, is laid out like an 18th-century herb and rose garden with every plant having an historical significance. Horsham Museum is a totally positive experience and I thoroughly recommend it.

## Other eccentricities

### FIELD PLACE

Percy Bysshe Shelley (*1792-1822*), poet and radical, was born at Field Place, near Horsham. No public access unfortunately, but there is a Shelley Room in the Horsham Museum celebrating the fact. Percy was the eldest son and heir of a wealthy squire but was disinherited for writing a pamphlet called 'The Necessity of Atheism'. Shelley may have been moved by the Black Princess's poignant story to write his own drama (unfinished) in verse about an Indian enchantress abandoned by her lover in a strange land.

> *He came like a dream in the dawn of life,*
> *He fled like a shadow before its noon,*
> *He is gone, and my peace is turned to strife,*
> *And I wander and wane like a weary moon.*

And later:

> *I offer only*
> *That which I seek, some human sympathy*
> *In this mysterious island.*

## COWDRAY CASTLE

A gloomy, picturesque 16th-century Tudor ruin on the edge of Midhurst that looks the perfect setting for a Hammer Horror movie. Henry VIII gave it to Sir Anthony Browne after the dissolution of the Catholic church. The castle eventually passed to the eighth Viscount Montague, a descendent of Browne. Montague died in a boating accident in 1793 and a week later the house burnt to the ground. The estate passed onto the Viscount's sister who amazingly and co-incidentally then also drowned in a boating accident, with both her sons, in 1815. Strange but true!

## EBERNOE HORN FAIR

Annually, on St James' Day, July 25, a fair is held in the tiny hamlet of Ebernoe, 8 kilometres north of Petworth. A ram is roasted and a cricket match played between Ebernoe and a rival village. The ram's symbolic horns are then presented to whichever batsman knocks up the most runs (a weird ancient tradition connected with scoring, seduction and dressing up). For the more spiritually minded, Ebernoe Fair day is also when gardeners are reminded to do a different type of seed sowing and get their spring cabbages in.

## LEONARDSLEE GARDENS

Did you know there are hopping marsupials just south of Horsham? During the late 1880s, when Sir Edmund Loder laid out his 97-hectare Himalayan Eden at Leonardslee, he introduced antelopes, beavers, kangaroos and wallabies. Sadly, only the latter remain and do a very effective job of mowing the grass. A trip to Leonardslee, with its magnificent woodland gardens and lakes is unlike visiting any normal garden. There is a heightened sense of anticipation and fun in waiting to see a wallaby bounce across the landscape! Presently closed to the public.

---

**Getting there**                                   National grid ref. TQ178309

❯ Car: off the A24 London/Worthing and A264 Crawley/Tunbridge Wells road.

❯ Train: National rail services from London/Victoria, Brighton and Chichester.

❯ Bus: National Express from Victoria coach station.

❯ Useful website: **www.horshammuseum.org**

# A BIGGER BANG

## LEWES

**Where is it?**

Tucked into the folds of the South Downs, inland from the port of Newhaven and 12 kilometres from the city of Brighton, Lewes is the county town of East Sussex. Rich in history, boasting a Norman castle, a handsome collection of Tudor, Georgian and Victorian buildings, a crown court and prison, a winding river with working wharves, an ancient (still functioning) brewery and a classic Georgian High Street, Lewes appears to be a comfortable, respectable and above all, calm place to be.

**What is it?**

Every year Lewesians gather together with thousands of excited visitors to celebrate the anniversary of November 5, 1605, when Guy Fawkes and 12 other Catholic conspirators, led by Robert Catesby, attempted to overthrow the Protestant government, but failed. As well as celebrating the execution of Guy Fawkes, Lewes uses bonfire or 'bone fire', night to commemorate the town's 17 Protestant Martyrs. They had been burnt at the stake in Lewes during the reign of 'Bloody' Queen Mary, between 1555 and 1557, because they refused to acknowledge Rome and the Pope as their supreme spiritual authority.

The mixing up of these two events and the strong Protestant sentiments in Lewes at the time, gradually helped establish the roots of the traditions seen in the modern incarnation of the celebrations. Bonfire Night in Lewes is the wildest imaginable! The true significance of Guy Fawkes Night and his fiendish plot may have faded, but 21st-century Lewes remains the country's capital of the riotous bonfire party. Today, the festival has little to do with either religion or politics and is far more about having a great pyrotechnic night out.

Since it began in 1605, the celebration has gradually evolved into a weird Molotov cocktail of historical cross-dressing and the most bizarre and impressive firework party in the country. On November 5, Lewes stirs from its middle-class slumbers and is magically transformed into a pagan and frenzied place of danger – a town besieged by explosions, raging fires and the pungent smell of tar and sulphur. This usually calm and conventional community metamorphoses into a seemingly wild and insane mob of atavistic conspirators, re-enacting ancient blood-letting with primeval fervour.

**What else should I know?**

Frustrated by James I's failure to re-establish Catholicism in England when he came to the throne in 1603, the Gunpowder plotters planned to blow up the Houses of Parliament, killing the king and his entire Protestant government. In the ensuing chaos, they hoped to seize power and install a Roman Catholic monarch. However, the plot failed; Guido 'Guy' Fawkes, the explosives expert, was caught putting the final touches to his masterplan, arrested and tortured until he had confessed the names of his comrades, then was executed along with them. In the patriotic and anti-Catholic frenzy that followed their execution, English Catholics were ostracised and persecuted in an ongoing religious struggle that was to last for centuries.

The Protestant Establishment exploited this religious propaganda coup to its full. Anti-papist sentiments were given legal and free expression when an act of parliament, passed in January 1606, proclaimed an annual holiday on November 5. Gunpowder Treason Day, as Guy Fawkes' Day was originally known, became an official holiday in the Church of England calendar for the next 250 years. The festival was to celebrate and to thank God for rescuing England from the clutches of the Pope and the Roman Catholic Church. Special thanksgiving services and prayers were held in parish churches across the country. The army fired off canons, congregations rang their church bells, large bonfires were lit and effigies of the Pope were publicly burnt.

### Who organises it?

Today, there are seven highly competitive and territorial bonfire societies who organise the Lewes event: Borough, Cliffe, Commercial Square, Nevill Juvenile, Southover, South Street and Waterloo. It is deadly serious – you can't just join these clubs, you have to be invited and vetted. Each society has bonfire 'boys and girls' who organise fundraising and recruitment throughout the year. On the night itself, each group holds its own brilliant torch-lit parade and tries to out-do the others with their fancy dress parades, bonfires and firework displays.

The climax of the evening is the Grand United Procession. Brandishing flaming torches and fired up by mass hysteria, alcohol, political sloganeering and pyromania, the bonfire societies parade the entire length of Lewes waving banners and crying 'No Popery'. Recalling past events when the celebrations got out of control and violent revellers disguised themselves to escape recognition and arrest, each group dresses up in a dazzling array of costumes ranging from Native American Indians and Mongol warriors to porno vicars and customs men.

Accompanied by colourful marching bands, they make their way through the streets, up the High Street to the crest of the hill and the town's war memorial. Here, surrounded by thousands of spectators, they lay wreaths and solemnly pay tribute to those who lost their lives in the two World Wars and subsequent conflicts. The occasion is marked with a two-minute silence and the plangent sounding of the Last Post.

Then, dragging giant effigies of the Pope, Guy Fawkes and other contemporary political 'bad guys' towards their fates, the pageants proceed to their own individual bonfire sites and firework displays on the outskirts of town, and proceed to party. Photographs of the event are displayed in the High Street shop windows a few days later.

If you're not staying for the party, get out of town! Although today's celebrations are highly organised and safe events compared with the rioting, tar-burning and street-fighting dangers of bygone days, if you don't want to stay, leave Lewes early. Throughout the day police restrict parking in the town and begin closing off roads. Traders board up their windows, restaurateurs close early and the locals seal up their letter-boxes and lock in their pets. At about 5 o'clock in the afternoon, all routes in and out of Lewes are blocked off completely and the main procession streets cleared of any remaining cars. At the same time, thousands of bonfire aficionados begin arriving by special trains. Although well controlled, the town begins to take on a siege mentality as the party builds up a head of steam.

### Why visit it?

For sheer atavistic excitement; first-timers beware! It's a long evening so wear warm, waterproof clothes and bring some cheering food and drink along. There are street vendors but it's very difficult to move through the crowds to reach them. Most of the pubs are closed. The ones that do stay open are impossible to get into and the bouncers are ready for trouble-makers!

Here are a few house-rules. Don't bring your own fireworks because the police will either confiscate them or arrest you for letting them off. Arrive early, find a good spot on the High Street and don't move until the main procession is over. Don't bring small children, pets or pushchairs and if you suffer with asthma, claustrophobia or other such conditions, come with friends who will look after you if you have any problems. Bring lots of loose change because all the societies are fundraising and will keep waving large collecting buckets under your nose. Keep your wits about you at all times, and try to stay close to whoever you're with because once you become separated, it will be impossible to find each other again.

The party continues well into the early hours and even if it's raining, spirits are difficult to dampen. For the Eccentric Tourist, Lewes Bonfire Night is a must.

## Other eccentricities

### DRUIDS GALORE

Druid activity and pagan spirituality in Lewes are alive and well. The soft sensuous curves of the South Downs reveal the great buttocks and breasts of the Earth-Goddess Isis and the River Ouse winds its way through her open thighs into Lewes and the sea of creation (or something nuts like that). Modern Druidry focuses on a love of nature, expressing spirituality through ancient Celtic (commonsense) traditions celebrating the cycle of seasons. The Long Man of Wilmington (*see p. 47*) is a popular pagan venue and the South Downs in general provide lots of healing energy. Walk the Downs around Lewes and you have a 95% chance of seeing Celtic shenanigans. The head honcho of the Druids lives in Lewes and is a well-respected international speaker on the subject.

### MONKS HOUSE

Virginia Woolf (*1882-1941*) and her husband Leonard bought Monks House in Rodmell (a small, gloomy, weather-boarded house outside Lewes, now owned by the National Trust) as a holiday cottage in 1919. They moved there full-time after being bombed out of their London home in 1940. By London standards, life in the countryside was bleak and Monks House was cold, damp and miserable. Psychological illness and depression made life unbearable for Virginia and in 1941 she killed herself. She left letters for her husband and her sister Vanessa (*see page 21*), took a final walk to the Ouse, filled her pockets with heavy stones and drowned herself. No laughs here I'm afraid. Virginia Woolf's final novel, *Between the Acts* was completed just before her death, when she believed she had lost her ability to write and was going mad. It has been described as the longest suicide note in the English language.

**Getting there**    National grid ref. TQ415093
- Car: on the A27 between Brighton and Eastbourne.
- Train: National rail services from London/Victoria, Brighton and Eastbourne.
- Bus: frequent services from Brighton and Eastbourne.
- Useful website: **www.lewesbonfirecouncil.org.uk**

# AIRMAN'S GRAVE

## Where is it?

In a quiet hollow on open heathy slopes in the Ashdown Forest, just outside the village of Nutley, below tracks leading down from the Crowborough Road. It stands near where autumn gentians bloom and only metres away from the end of the village lanes as they merge in with the forest. There is a wide grassy track running past and an atmosphere of peace and tranquillity embraces the entire site.

## What is it?

The Airman's Grave is a low walled stone-built enclosure, maybe 10 metres square and stands on the exact spot where a Wellington Bomber from 142 Squadron crashed in 1941, killing all six of its crew. On the night of July 3 the aircraft was limping home from a bombing raid on Cologne, flying on only one engine, the pilot desperately searching for an airfield close to the south coast to land the damaged plane. Appalling weather conditions made it impossible to find a suitable landing site and it nose-dived deep into the forest. Whether deliberately or accidentally, the pilot just managed to avoid crashing into Nutley itself. Had the plane come down a few hundred metres nearer, it would have been a catastrophe for the village.

Only one body was ever recovered intact: that of the rear gunner Len Saunders. The other young men were: Harry Vidler (captain and pilot), Vic Sutton (co-pilot), Stan Hathaway (gunner), Wilf Brooks (observer) and Arthur Cave (wireless operator) but too little of them remained for burial or cremation. All of the crew were young, in their early to mid-20s.

### Who made it?

A few years after the tragedy, the co-pilot's mother came to live in Nutley. It was she, along with the other mothers of the men who died, who decided to create a permanent memorial to their sons. In 1945, the forest rangers reported that a wooden cross had been erected on the crash site, planted with wild flowers and surrounded by a wooden fence to keep the sheep and deer at bay. Although the grave infringed local by-laws, the authorities were sympathetic and the memorial remained. The grave was cared for by forest rangers as well as Mrs Sutton.

In 1954, a permanent white stone cross was erected and in 1971 the wooden fence was replaced by a sheltering wall of local stone built by two local rangers, identified only as A.J. and P.J. Their initials, along with the date are inscribed on the right-hand side of the entrance. In 1992, ex-RAF navigator and commercial airline pilot Frank Wilson, a resident of nearby Duddleswell, had a memorial plaque erected on the stone wall. Under the appreciative care of the forest rangers, the planted trees and flowers have matured and the Airman's Grave has evolved into a place of pilgrimage and reflection.

### Why visit it?

Every year on Remembrance Sunday, the living gather together at the Airman's Grave to remember the young airmen who were killed, and all those other service men and women who have died, and continue to die, for their country. Relatives of those young airmen reunite here every year and reflect on the sacrifice they made nearly 60 years ago. Just before 11 o'clock in the morning, the service from the Cenotaph in Whitehall is relayed over the radio. Big Ben signals in the beginning of the two-minute silence, the radio is switched off and the silence observed. Watched over by representatives from the British Legion, local bystanders, a few walkers with dogs, children and riders with horses, the custom has become firmly established in the community. Wreaths are laid, the Last Post is played and the local vicar leads the occasion: 'We will remember them.'

In recent years, as the service is concluding, Frank Wilson has flown over the site in his private aircraft with an open cockpit and dropped thousands of paper poppy petals on the proceedings below. Petals flutter down from the sky in a red cloud, gently colouring the grave, the surrounding forest and the heads and shoulders of the gathered crowd.

### What other Airmen's Graves are there?

At the other end of the county, there is a memorial to a German pilot just north of North Marden and east of the Hampshire border on the South Downs Way (OS reference SU824170). The memorial is to Captain (Hauptmann) Joseph Oestermann (*1915-40*), one of the first Germans to be killed during Hitler's airborne attacks on England. He had been flying a Junkers Ju88 bomber on August 13 1940 (the first day of the Battle of Britain) and was shot down, probably by Pilot-Officer Mayers of 601 Squadron from nearby Tangmere.

And in Boxgrove Cemetery (on the A27 just east of Chichester) is the grave of Billy Fiske (*1911-41*), the first American citizen to be killed in action fighting for Britain. He was a fighter pilot.

### Other eccentricities

#### ASHDOWN FOREST

It would be unforgivable to come to the Ashdown Forest and ignore A.A. Milne, Christopher Robin and Winnie the Pooh. After the reflective visit to the Airmen's Grave it could be fun to invoke E.H. Shepherd's charming illustrations of teddy bear Pooh and go looking for some of Milne's more identifiable locations (all based on real sites). Poohsticks Bridge, for example, is Posingford Bridge, built in 1907 and repaired by the Disney Corporation after Milne's widow sold the rights in Pooh to Disney in 1961.

## THE GHOST RAILWAY

The abandoned Ouse Valley Railway was supposed to run between the southern end of Balcombe Viaduct on the main London to Brighton line, through Lindfield, Sheffield Park to Uckfield, possibly later continuing to St Leonards and the south coast. The 32-kilometre line was begun but mysteriously never finished. Work started on the first stretch to Uckfield in May 1866 and then stopped abruptly in February 1867 after flooding and an economic slump in the Victorian railway boom. Despite no trains ever running along the line, some paranormal fruitcakes still claim to hear steam whistles (maybe in their heads they can)!

Almost 140 years further down the line you can still find small traces of the railway that never was: brick abutments near Balcombe Viaduct where a bridge was to be widened; embankments either side of the road from Borde Hill Gardens to Haywards Heath Golf Club; the eastern cutting which would have led to a short tunnel and is now an ornamental lake, but they are all rapidly returning to nature. What is strangely certain is that had this line been completed, the East Grinstead to Lewes line (part of which became the Bluebell Railway) would never have been built, and we wouldn't be hearing steam trains in the Ouse Valley today.

**Getting there**             National grid ref. TQ442275
- Car: off the A22 between Maresfield and Forest Row on the B2026.
- Train: nearest station Uckfield, 4-mile (7-kilometre) walk.
- Bus: services from East Grinstead to Nutley.
- Useful website: **www.ashdownforest.co.uk/Places/nutley.htm**

# THE CHATTRI

## PATCHAM

**Where is it?**

The Chattri is miles from anywhere and quite difficult to find! More precisely, it is located north of Brighton between the villages of Patcham and Pyecombe, hidden away from busy roads in a peaceful fold of the South Downs. The easiest starting point is the car park at Jack and Jill, the two windmills in the hamlet of Clayton. Once you have picked up the trail for The Chattri, displayed on marker posts to the south of the windmills, it is an energetic one-and-a-half-hour's walk. This takes you around the local golf course and provides spectacular views of the surrounding downland. Take refreshments with you, as there are no chintzy tearooms en route.

**What is it?**

The Chattri is a grand white marble pavilion, rising surreally from its incongruous setting, a piece of oriental architecture reminiscent of Raj India and the flamboyant domes of Brighton Pavilion. It is in fact a cenotaph honouring the Sikh and Hindu soldiers who died fighting for Britain during the First World War (you remember, the war that was to end all wars). 'Chattri' is the Hindi, Punjabi and Urdu word for umbrella.

It is built on the site where Sikh and Hindu soldiers were cremated on funeral pyres during the war (the Muslim dead were buried at the Shah Jehan Mosque at Woking, Surrey). Their ashes were then taken and scattered at sea in accordance with their religious tradition[1]. An inscription in Hindi, Punjabi, Urdu and English reads:

> To the memory of all Indian soldiers who gave their lives for their King-Emperor in the Great War, this monument, erected on the site of the funeral pyre where Hindus and Sikhs who died in hospital at Brighton passed through the fire, is in grateful admiration and brotherly affection dedicated.

Unlike the modern simplicity of many European war memorials, most notably characterised by Sir Edwin Lutyens' Cenotaph in Whitehall, The Chattri celebrates eastern forms and decoration. It is 2.7 metres wide and 8.8 metres high, occupying a grassy slope within a hedged enclosure. On the cross axis are four radiating paths planted with heather and hawthorn. The tomb sits on an elevated stone platform facing south towards the sprawl of Brighton. The pavilion has an octagonal base from which eight decorative pillars rise up to support a hollow dome, or 'umbrella'. This dome has bands of engraved ornamentation circling its roof and is crowned with a finial. The Chattri is a more sober interpretation of orientalism than the flamboyant and theatrical Brighton Pavilion with its fanciful and ostentatious chinoiserie. It was designed as an imperial monument both to bolster a disintegrating empire and to help cement a lasting bond between Britain and India. The political significance of The Chattri was reinforced by the attendance of the Prince of Wales at its official unveiling on February 21 1921.

## Who made it?

This startling edifice was designed in 1920 by a young Indian architect called E.C. Henriques, about whom very little is known, overseen by British architect Sir Samuel Swinton Jacob (*1841-1917*). Although not considered outstanding, Jacob was involved in the design of many new buildings under construction in New Delhi and had extensive knowledge of Indian architectural traditions. The construction of The Chattri was jointly funded by Brighton Corporation and the Indian

---

**1.** *The official website www.chattri.com gives the numbers of soldiers cremated as 53 but you may find conflicting numbers given by different sources.*

Office, with Brighton Corporation undertaking the responsibility for maintenance and repairs.

## What else should I know?

When World War I broke out, India was part of the British Empire, and Indian infantry divisions started arriving on the Western Front from October 1914. In total, India contributed over a one and a half million men towards the war effort in Europe, of which 826,868 were combatants. By the end of the slaughter, 113,743 Indian soldiers were reported either dead, wounded or missing. Of those injured, 12,000 were brought back to Britain for medical treatment in temporary hospitals. Four such makeshift hospitals were set up along the south coast, three of which were in Brighton and Hove: the Brighton Work House, renamed the Kitchener General Indian Hospital (now Brighton General Hospital), York Place School, the Dome and the Corn Exchange on the Royal Pavilion Estate. It is said that Indian soldiers were housed in the Royal Pavilion in the mistaken belief that they would feel more at home. As most of the men came from poor, rural villages it is unlikely that the Pavilion's oriental domes and fabulous decoration offered much that was familiar!

On Monday December 14, 1914, a drab cold day, the Brighton Gazette reported emotional scenes in the town as 345 wounded Indian soldiers arrived at Brighton Railway Station. The special train with its heroic passengers was met by the Mayor, the Chief Constable and representatives of the Red Cross and St John's Ambulance. The injured soldiers were then transported by ambulance to the hospitals. Sadly, despite the best efforts of nursing staff, not all the soldiers survived their ordeal.

## Why visit it?

During the 1930s, The Chattri was neglected while municipal and governmental bodies squabbled about who was supposed to be looking after it. It was even used for target practice when the area was requisitioned by the military during World War II, but in 1951 the British Legion took it over, and The Chattri's dignity was gradually restored.

Since 2000 there has been an annual ceremony of remembrance, a tradition revived by a local Sikh teacher, Davinder Dhillon. Every year, on the third Sunday in June, the Patcham Branch of The Royal British Legion organise an emotional pilgrimage across the windswept Downs to The Chattri. The combination of poignancy, startled and curious walkers and the isolated setting give the proceedings a surreal edge. Marchers lay wreaths of poppies, say prayers, play the Last Post and remember the dead. Those attending the ceremony include representatives from the Indian High Commission, local dignitaries, war veterans from the Indian Army, members of the Royal Air Force, the British Army, the Police and local mourners who wish to pay their respects at this incongruous memorial hidden in the Downs. Tea is served afterwards at the Gardner Centre, in the grounds of the University of Sussex at Falmer.

Do take a walk up there one day. Enjoy the peaceful countryside but stop for a while and reflect on those poor Indian soldiers who died so far away from their own homes and families.

## Other eccentricities

### CLAYTON TUNNEL

An absurdly castellated folly at the front entrance, with battlemented turrets and arrow slits, it is best viewed from the bridge on the A273 Brighton road, near the hamlet of Clayton, not far from Hasssocks. The cottage sitting between the two turrets is more recent and the occupants are subjected to continual subterranean railway rumblings. It is most famous for a terrible crash in 1861, when two steam trains collided inside the tunnel, killing 23 passengers and injuring 176.

---

**Getting there**                                    National grid ref. TQ304111

- Car: access for annual service only. As you enter Brighton on the A23, take the A27 towards Lewes. At second roundabout (with slip road to Lewes) take the north exit into Braypool Lane and follow the signs.
- Bus: frequent services to Pyecombe for energetic walkers.
- Useful website: **www.chattri.com**

# MERIDIAN MONOLITH

## PEACEHAVEN

### Where is it?

Peacehaven is on the congested A259 south coast road east of Brighton, situated between the olde-world village charms of Rottingdean, the busy, scruffy industrial port of Newhaven and the glorious South Downs. The monument itself sits on the cliff edge, sandwiched between the suburban bungalows at the junction of Horsham Avenue and the sea. Turned slightly askew to the edge of the rock face on which it stands and gazing stoically across the English Channel, it takes the visitor completely by surprise when first stumbled upon.

### What is it?

The Meridian Monument is an imposing white decorative obelisk, about 3.5 metres high, its pinnacle crowned with a globe. It celebrates Peacehaven's unique position on the zero-degree longitude meridian line. This imaginary and invisible navigational line circles the globe running from the North Pole to the South, slicing through the Royal Observatory at Greenwich, then southwards via Lewes and Peacehaven, before disappearing out to sea on its journey around the planet. It is from this line that all distance is measured and from which the world sets its clocks. Braced against a bitter sea wind, it is heart-warming, if not a little surreal, to read a weather-worn plaque giving precise distances from Peacehaven to faraway and romantic (if completely random) destinations such as Rangoon, Burma, 5,586 miles; Halifax, Nova Scotia, 2,893 miles; Canberra, Australia, 10,564 miles.

Standing alone on the cliffs, the monument makes a feeble nod to the tourist searching for Peacehaven's lost Art Deco aspirations. Built at a cost of £300, it was unveiled on August 10, 1935, the year of George V's Silver Jubilee, and dedicated to the king a year later. Since its original inauguration, it has been moved inland twice because of land erosion to the cliffs on which it stands.

The seats around the edifice are usually empty and the two ornamental drinking fountains on either side of the obelisk are dry: indicative perhaps of the English seaside holiday destination in decline, alongside Peacehaven's unfulfilled ambitions.

## Who made it?

The monument, and indeed Peacehaven itself, was the brainwave of Charles Neville (*1881-1960*), a British-born but Canadian-raised adventurer of slightly dubious character who, in 1914, started buying agricultural land along the coast at knockdown prices. His aim was to develop a dream seaside resort. Neville was a natural entrepreneur: advertising extensively; running high profile press campaigns; devising numerous competitions to win building plots as well as ready-built gift houses. He advertised Peacehaven as a seaside paradise but, in reality, conditions were pretty sombre and the site, with its rough tracks and rudimentary services, looked more like an American frontier town than a dream haven. Despite all this he succeeded in attracting undaunted pioneer settlers wanting to buy their own little piece of England and build a new life in a garden city by the sea.

## When was Peacehaven built?

When the town was first envisaged in 1914, the farmland along the windswept cliffs was cleared, surveyed and divided up on a grid pattern into thousands of building plots. Regular intersecting roads were marked out running east to west and dirt avenues marked running north to south. Although World War I interrupted work, Neville ran a national competition to choose a name for his dream town. First prize was £100, with 50 second prizes of £50 building plots. The winning name, chosen from more than 80,000 suggestions was New Anzac on Sea, in honour of the Australian and New Zealand Army Corps which ran a training camp in the area. However, because of negative associations with the later disastrous and tragic defeat at Gallipoli in 1916, the name was quietly changed to Peacehaven in 1917. The first house was completed in 1921. There were originally four monoliths, two at either end of the town, celebrating the gateway to this brave new world. Unfortunately a lorry destroyed one in 1900 so now there are only three.

Although Neville tried to monopolise house building through his estate company, he failed. Many of the prizewinners never actually developed the land they won, some settlers claimed squatter's rights on unclaimed plots and others built only basic shacks. There was no school or police force, only an unreliable electricity supply and hardly any sanitation, so development was ramshackle and chaotic. On top of this there was a national scandal when it was revealed that a legal fee of over £3.00 had been levied on each win. Yet despite these setbacks, lack of capital and high unemployment rates in post-war Britain, by 1924 the population of Peacehaven had grown to 3,000. There were grandiose plans for railways, piers, promenades and pavilions, tree-lined avenues, tea gardens and numerous other amenities but sadly these all failed to materialise. Eventually the council compulsorily purchased many of the remaining plots in order to complete the town.

**Why visit it?**

Peacehaven is an early 20th-century enterprise that went wrong. However, despite a lack of infrastructure, the town continued to grow and prosper and helped fulfil the ambitions of brave pioneers and returning war heroes wanting a new start, cheap land and a home of their own. It was badly let down by lack of cohesive town planning and inadequate building controls. Its layout disregards the natural contours of the land, lacks communal parks and gardens and has no overall design vision. It's a town-planners' byword for haphazard architectural urban sprawl.

For many, however, it is the very combination of the coastal site, quaint little self-build cottages, mock Tudor bungalows and other bizarre mixtures of style that gives Peacehaven its own eccentric and unique charm. Amidst this clutter sits a monument celebrating the entrepreneurial spirit of the time and an accidentally shared geographic position with the Greenwich Observatory.

## Other eccentricities

### HEATHY BROW

This is the oldest (now listed) building in Peacehaven and was a shepherd's cot or shelter. It existed well before Neville's dream seaside resort and forms part of a private house in Stanley Road.

### SALTDEAN LIDO

Charles Neville also developed Saltdean (halfway between Peacehaven and Brighton), with its iconic 1930s Lido and Ocean Hotel. The hotel became a Butlin's holiday camp in the 1950s and then apartments. The Lido, undoubtedly influenced by Mendelsohn's De La Warr Pavilion in Bexhill, remains a public swimming pool and is a classic example of lido architecture. Currently closed due to renovation work.

### ROTTINGDEAN

Genteel picture-postcard village with famous cultural connections, just outside the brighter lights of Brighton. Notable luvvies, including Sir Edward Burne-Jones (*1833-98*), Rudyard Kipling (*1865-1936*) and Enid Bagnold (*1889-1981*), all lived and worked here for part of their lives. For best bracing walks, take the undercliff path to Brighton (about 8 kilometres), which is wonderful in all weathers but particularly storms.

**Getting there**  National grid ref. TQ388016
- ◗ Car: on the A259 coast road between Brighton and Newhaven.
- ◗ Train: nearest station Newhaven, 2-mile (4-kilometre) walk.
- ◗ Bus: frequent services from Brighton and Eastbourne.
- ◗ Useful website: **www.geograph.org.uk/photo/30914**

# BLUEBELL RAILWAY

## SHEFFIELD PARK

**Where is it?**

The Bluebell Railway runs along the border straddling East and West Sussex, between Sheffield Park, Horsted Keynes and Kingscote. The best point to join the Bluebell is at Sheffield Park station situated on the A275 East Grinstead to Lewes road, north of its junction with the A272.

Horsted Keynes, the intermediate station at the centre of the line, is a mile and a half north-west of the village itself, right in the heart of the Sussex countryside. It is 8 kilometres from Haywards Heath, 9 kilometres from East Grinstead and about 18 kilometres from Gatwick.

**What is it?**

The Bluebell Railway takes its name from the swathe of bluebells clothing the railway embankments during spring and was the first standard-gauge, all-steam passenger railway in the world to be preserved for posterity. It now operates as a living museum. The line, stations, steam locomotives and rolling stock were all rescued from the scrap heap in the late 1950s, just before the great age of Victorian steam travel hit the buffers on British mainline railways in 1968. The Bluebell first opened its ticket office to the public in 1960, shortly after the East Grinstead to Lewes line closed. This was part of a massive programme of controversial closures to the national network carried out by British Railways' hatchetman Dr Richard Beeching in the late 1950s and early 60s. Since then the 14-kilometre stretch of line has developed into one of the most eccentric tourist attractions in Sussex, managed and run largely by volunteers. For train aficionados with fond folk memories of steam travel, the Bluebell Railway has become a nostalgic, atmospheric and romantic journey back through time.

The construction of the railways was a magnificent enterprise and in itself sums up the dynamism, grandeur and self-confidence of the Victorian age. When the network was introduced across Britain by entrepreneurial business pioneers, it opened up the country and became possible for ordinary people to travel between most places in a single day, without an overnight stay en route. It was an exciting, affordable, quick and comfortable way of travelling – a new, superior mode of transport that immediately killed off its rivals. There was of course suspicion and dissent from many quarters and fierce battles fought between railway companies and landowners over land acquisition but the merits of rail travel were obvious and, by 1850, trains were an established institution. Railway travel for pleasure quickly became an affordable and commonplace experience and railway excursions became fashionable.

## Who made it?

Miss Madge Bessemer of Chailey and the Bluebell Railway Preservation Society are responsible for its continued existence. When British Railways first put forward their plan to close the Lewes to East Grinstead line in 1954, it was vigorously opposed by a group of local residents, led by Miss Bessemer. The stretch of track was part of the old London, Brighton and South Coast Railway line. The line's original Act of 1877 contained a legal requirement to run four trains a day in each direction, so the local activists managed to stave off its inevitable closure for a couple of years by challenging the legality of the decision. But after four years of bitter feuding, and taking their legal challenge to the House of Commons and through a public enquiry, Goliath won the battle and the line finally closed on March 17, 1958.

Having lost their war, the enthusiastic and hard-working pioneers re-grouped, raised money, bought as much of the line as they could afford from British Railways and reopened it as a steam museum. The three stations have each been restored to reflect different periods in the railway's history and once you've bought a ticket, you can travel up and down the line, getting on and off different trains at different stations as many times as you wish. Sheffield Park has the general Victorian ambience of The London, Brighton and South Coast Railway in its heyday, Horsted Keynes emulates the style of National Railways between the wars, and Kingscote echoes early British Railways in the 1950s.

## Why visit it?

Back in the spring of 1959, the original intention of the Bluebell Railway branch-line preservationists was to re-open the Lewes to East Grinstead line in its entirety and run a commercial service. When those plans fell through, the idea of a steam railway heritage museum was a compromise but an excellent one.

The Bluebell Railway is a charmingly romanticised reincarnation of what it felt like to be a railway traveller on a steam train in the 1950s. And you don't need trainspotting inclinations to enjoy the experience – which is a sort of Thomas The Tank Engine extravaganza of endless summers, with a sleepy and beguiling atmosphere. The actual journey of childhood nostalgia between Sheffield Park and Kingscote stations only takes about half an hour in real time, but the Bluebell experience is a truly eccentric excursion to savour to the full and you can easily make a day of it.

The Bluebell journey isn't exactly intrepid rail travel but it does re-create a harmless and wholesome mood of dream-like quality, which is totally absorbing. The puffing steam engines; the chugging ride through pretty Sussex countryside; the drivers, porters and engineers dressed in authentic period uniforms; the pungent smell of coal and soot (relive the joy of hot ash in your eyes and up your nose), the sound of screeching wheels and ear-shattering steam whistles; the beautifully restored engines and carriages; the railway stations with their ephemera and railway posters – it's not surprising it's in such demand as a setting for period films and heart-warming retro TV series.

## Other eccentricities

### PILTDOWN MAN

Piltdown is the site of the best anthropological conspiracy scandal ever. For 40 years, a bunch of fossilised head-bones discovered in gravel pits on the outskirts of Piltdown were believed to be the skull and lower jaw of an evolutionary 'missing-link' between ape and man and prove Darwin's theory of evolution conclusively. Piltdown Man or *Eoanthropus Dawsoni* became the Holy Grail of fossil hunters after fragments of his skull were discovered by Charles Dawson in 1912 (solicitor and amateur geologist with an uncanny knack of making spectacular discoveries). The bones were given the academic thumbs-up by Arthur Woodward, keeper of the geological department at the British Museum, reconstructed into a skull and fooled the scientific establishment for decades.

In 1938, Sir Arthur Keith, the much-acclaimed anthropologist and expert in human fossils, unveiled a memorial stone to mark the site and proclaimed the following:

> *So long as man is interested in his long past history, in the vicissitudes which our early forerunners passed through, and the varying fare which overtook them, the name of Charles Dawson is certain of remembrance. We do well to link his name to this picturesque corner of Sussex – the scene of his discovery. I have now the honour of unveiling this monolith dedicated to his memory.*

The forgery was finally exposed in 1953, when advances in scientific date testing confirmed the fake. Piltdown Man was found to be a composite hoax of human skull, orangutan and chimpanzee – all stained to look old. Nobody can prove for certain that Dawson was solely responsible for perpetrating the Piltdown practical joke but it was a good one!

---

**Getting there**                                    National grid ref. TQ403237
- Car: on the A275 East Grinstead to Lewes road, just off the A275.
- Train: nearest station Haywards Heath then bus.
- Bus: regular services to East Grinstead, then join Bluebell's special bus to Kingscote.
- Useful website: **www.bluebell-railway.co.uk**

# HOLLYWOOD-BY-SEA

## SHOREHAM BEACH

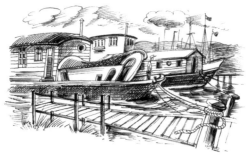

### Where are they?

Shoreham-by-Sea is halfway between Brighton and Worthing, bang in the middle of an exceedingly ugly stretch of industrial ribbon development that meanders along the coast road between the two centres. Shoreham's fortunes have ebbed and flowed over the centuries but its prosperity has always relied on the sea. The town was first established by Norman conquerors towards the end of the 11th century and by the Middle Ages was a successful and important port and ship-building centre. Despite a continually changing coastline, problems with moving shingle banks, serious erosion and encroaching floods, the town flourished. This early prosperity is clearly demonstrated by the grandeur of St Mary de Haura, the large Norman church in the centre of the old town and in the few remaining 18th-century merchant houses. Although Shoreham was virtually wiped out in a series of storms at the beginning of the 18th century, by the middle of the century it had recovered well enough to be supplying London with 200,000 tons of oysters and scallops a year, transported daily. Today, the harbour remains the largest commercial port operating between Dover and Portsmouth.

At one end of the town is a rusty steel footbridge, which takes you over a muddy estuary to Shoreham Beach, a massive shingle spit, now entirely covered with flats and bungalows. At first sight, there is little to suggest that Shoreham offers the thrill-seeker anything other than the appealing dinginess of a small provincial seaside; but take a closer look.

## What are they?

Moored up along the southern bank of the muddy estuary of the River Adur is an extraordinary colony of assorted houseboats, some dating back to well before World War II.

This unconventional and eclectic fleet includes a 100-year-old wooden schooner, several tugs, an old steam yacht, a 1922 Royal Navy Torpedo boat, a mini-fleet of renovated industrial barges, an amazing and brightly coloured floating metal sculpture combining parts of a bus with parts of a barge, and at least one scrap-metal rendition of Noah's Ark. Shoreham's floating homesteads are lovingly created, uplifting and unconventional works of art. They reflect the town's personality – quirky and creative but with attitude.

## Who made them?

Shoreham's bohemian heritage dates back to the early 20th century, when the town's shingle beach became a popular theatre and film colony. Artists and technicians keen to find work in the burgeoning new film industry flocked to Shoreham, poor but optimistic, and put up in converted railway carriages, old barges and improvised shacks

Following the horrors of World War I, people desperately needed to find work and create a new start and it was relatively easy to set up home in an old railway carriage, or makeshift barge. As town planning became more regulated, many of these temporary one-storey dwellings, or bungalows, became permanent fixtures, and so Shoreham Beach became established.

## Why them?

Larger resorts such as Eastbourne, Brighton and Worthing have managed to survive the changing tastes of post-war holidaymakers but Shoreham languishes in their shadows and has taken on the shabby demeanour of a seaside town in decline. It is not an obvious first choice for a good time and on a cold bleak day you may doubt your sanity or indeed this guide-book, but persevere. The houseboat colony is a bizarre and unconventional settlement well worth a visit. Remember, though, these are people's homes, so respect their privacy when viewing.

## Sunny Shoreham

Brighton and Hove were both associated with early film and cinema and in 1913 The Sunny South Film Company was formed and started making films from Shoreham. The natural light in the area was considered excep-tionally well suited for daylight productions and described by The Prospect Film Company in their prospectus as:

> Undoubtedly the Los Angeles of English production, with a pure and clean light, probably unrivalled by any other place in England.

Several other studios were built (among them The Progress Film Company, The Shoreham Beach Film Studio and The Sealight Film Company), and many films, including the first UK production of *Little Dorrit* (1920), and *The Mayor of Casterbridge* (1921) were made at Shoreham. *The Mayor of Casterbridge* was the first film to be made entirely on location, and the author of the book on which it was based, Thomas Hardy, was on hand as an adviser, despite believ-ing (in typically gloomy fashion) that film was just another pointless passing fad.

The film industry was developing quickly and studios moved, went bust, merged with each other and changed hands fairly rapidly. The collapse of the industry in Shoreham started in 1922, when The Shoreham Film Studio was destroyed by fire and The Progress Film Company went into liquidation. All that remains now as a testament to Shoreham's brief encounter with the glamour of movie-making is a memorial plaque on the wall of the church hall built on the site of the Shoreham Film Studio.

The show may have left town but many of the artistic settlers stayed on. It was they who formed the bedrock of Shoreham's creative commu-nity and houseboat colony.

## Other eccentricities

### LANCING COLLEGE CHAPEL

The countryside outside Shoreham is dominated by the Adur River Valley, which at high tide is a wide lake. As the water recedes, the tidal inlet becomes a narrow tributary of murky water snaking its way back through the mud towards the sea. The wide expanse of vegetated marshland is a diverse wildlife habitat for birds, flora and fauna.

Above it all looms the massive Gothic Revival Chapel of Lancing College,[1] looking slightly too big for the landscape it dominates. Lancing College was founded in 1848 by the Reverend Nathanial Woodard, the indefatigable educational entrepreneur, but the chapel was not begun until 1868 and is still unfinished. Claimed to be the largest school chapel in Europe, it was built by the father-and-son team of Richard Cromwell Carpenter (*1812-55*) and Richard Herbert Carpenter (*1841-93*), with their assistant William Slater, and is 53 metres high, with foundations that go down 21 metres. It is still missing the tower that the founder planned for it, which would have added yet another 53 metres to its height. It is said to have the second largest rose window in the country after York Minster, and contains the Reverend Woodard's tomb.

### SHOREHAM AIRPORT

To the west of the town is Shoreham Airport, the country's oldest licensed airfield. The first commercial flights took off from here to Deauville, France, in 1935. It is worth a visit to look at its gorgeous Art Deco terminal building, built between 1934 and 1936 by Stavers Hessell Tiltman (*1888-1968*). It still has many of its original features, and is a favourite location for period films and TV series.

Bungalow Town Halt, the railway station that originally served Shoreham airport, was opened in 1910, closed in 1933, re-opened two years later as Shoreham Airport Station, and closed for good in 1940.

---

**1.** *The chapel is open to the public every day between 10.00 and 16.00 and on Sunday between 12.00 and 16.00.*

## WORTHING

Worthing (west along the coast from Shoreham) was the first place in West Sussex where audiences paid to see films. When the seductively named Electric Theatre first opened its doors in 1911 (then part of an Edwardian leisure centre opposite Worthing Pier called the Kursaal), it was considered a technological marvel. Instantly successful, the Electric Theatre was refurbished, renamed and re-launched after World War I as The Dome. When it was first built the theatre was described as: 'A building without parallel in the kingdom'. As one of the oldest working cinemas left in the country, it remains a unique monument to film which we should all support by going there on wet Sunday afternoons, but please, no noisy sweet wrappers!

## BRIGHTON PAVILION

If you're in Raj mode or need luxurious yet eccentric shelter from the vicissitudes of English weather, head for the hedonistic lights of Brighton and the Royal Pavilion's pleasure domes (*see p. 28*). Fantasy India outside; Chinese opulence inside.

**Getting there** National grid ref. TQ215046
- ❯ Car: off the A27 between Lewes and Worthing, on the A259 coast road.
- ❯ Train: National rail services from London/Victoria, Brighton and Coastway.
- ❯ Bus: National Express from Victoria coach station and local services from Brighton and Worthing.
- ❯ Useful website: **www.shorehambysea.com**

# THE GREAT IHAM

## WINCHELSEA

**Where is it?**

Perched high and dry on a hill called Iham! More precisely Winchelsea is 5 kilometres inland from Rye near the East Sussex/Kent border and 3 kilometres inland from the shingle beaches of Pett Level. This ancient medieval town is on the western edge of Romney Marsh, high above low-lying wetlands on an elevated plateau which majestically dominates the surrounding landscape.

**What is it?**

Winchelsea's legacy is as a beautiful, unspoiled and unfinished example of medieval new town planning. The original layout of Winchelsea remains remarkably intact. It is set out on a regular grid pattern with the magnificent Church of St Thomas a Becket in pride of place at the centre. Originally there were 39 squares, divided up symmetrically by wide intersecting streets. In medieval times the houses would have been made primarily of timber. Substantial stone and brick buildings have gradually replaced those early settlements and what survives today is a romantic mixture of well-groomed Georgian and Victorian exteriors with the occasional 20th-century supplement.

In its heyday, Winchelsea was the principal seaport of Sussex, a Cinque port, and one of the most important in England. The sea would have lapped at the foot of the steep cliffs and there was a large, deep and sheltered natural harbour to the north – where the River Brede and caravan park now are. Yes, amazingly the town was a thriving and wealthy port – not marooned inland as it is today!

## Who made it?

During the 13th century this part of the south coast was eroding. The original town was badly flooded by a storm in 1236 and then again, more seriously, in 1250 and 1252. Finally, in 1287, there were freak and overpowering weather conditions which dramatically changed the whole coastline in the region. Some historians believe that subsidence or a subterranean earthquake may have caused a tsunami. Eyewitness accounts describe a red moon, hours of gale-force winds, a flooding high tide, with terrifying fiery crests on the huge waves, and then no ebb at all before another huge flood tide. This natural disaster flooded Romney Marsh as far north as Appledore and moved the mouth of the River Rother several miles westward along the coast from Romney to Rye. It inundated Old Winchelsea completely, and the old town now lies buried somewhere beneath the sea, about 5 kilometres south-east of where the new town now stands, possibly at Camber Sands.

New Winchelsea was established on a high and well-protected site, away from danger, shortly after the original town had been swallowed up. It was all made possible by royal patronage. The plots, some of which were never fully developed, were given to the inhabitants by Edward I in 1288 to help build a new town, after the destruction of their old one.

With its earth ramparts, ditches and dykes, reinforced town walls and massive gates, this new and fortified manifestation of Winchelsea must have seemed strategically and economically unassailable. But less than a century later, the sea had piled up shingle and was receding, the harbour had silted up and the town's tide of prosperity had turned. By the end of the 15th century, the town's life as a thriving port was over.

## Why visit it?

Partly as a lesson in hubris, to see how even the mighty can fall, partly to admire how the town has adapted gracefully to a diminished role, and partly to admire Winchelsea's great church. The grandeur of the Church of St Thomas a Becket reflects the bold aspirations of new Winchelsea when it was first established in the 1280s. No one is quite sure whether the building was never finished or if parts of it were destroyed during French raids. What remains, however, is a fascinating historical town and a beautiful church of great interest. There is a black Madonna, a Green Man and some fine Sussex marble figures reputed to have been rescued from Old Winchelsea church during the flood; one of these has his ankles crossed indicating he was a Knight Templar.

There are also some glorious stained glass windows designed by Douglas Strachan (1875-1950), the great Scottish stained glass artist. Commissioned as a memorial to World War I, they depict the themes of Land, Air, Fire and Sea. The latter window honours the men of the *Mary Stanford* lifeboat who died while on a rescue mission in 1928. Strachan's magnificent windows evoke thanksgiving for the victims of war, emphasising both the creative and destructive life forces in all humanity.

Close by the church is the museum, housed in the old courthouse, along with the armoury; a pub and a village shop which stocks local specialist food. Outside in the walled churchyard is the comedian Spike Milligan's grave. Look straight ahead from the church door, slightly to the left and you will find a Celtic cross. The Gaelic inscription on the cross apparently reads: '*I told you I was ill*' – a fitting epitaph to one of our great comic eccentrics.

Opposite the New Inn is 'Wesley's Tree' where the great Methodist John Wesley (1703-91), a great favourite in Winchelsea, preached his last sermon in the open air on October 7, 1790. It is not the actual ash tree, which blew down in 1927, but was grown from a seed of the original. Wesley noted in his journal,

> *I stood under a large tree and called to most of the inhabitants of the town 'the kingdom of heaven is at hand: repent and believe in the Gospel'. It seemed as if all that heard were, at the present, almost persuaded to be Christians.*

Amazingly enough, Wesley was linked, at least tangentially, to smuggling, Winchelsea's main industry after decline had set in. Wesley's daughter was engaged to the gallant Captain Henry Haddock, commander of the Rye revenue cutter, who was gunned down by smugglers off Dungeness. The last smuggler killed in England was allegedly Thomas Monk, a 'poor fiddler' of Winchelsea, on April 1, 1838 in a stand-off with coastguards.

### What else should I know?

Seven centuries ago Winchelsea was a wealthy and thriving harbour and a member of the Cinque or five Ports Confederation. The original Cinque ports were Hastings, Dover, Hythe, Romney and Sandwich. Winchelsea and Rye were affiliated later. The ports were obliged to provide ships, supplies and men for the Royal fleet and to help protect the south-east coast against invasion, to transport the King and court overseas when required and to protect the fisheries in the North Sea. The payback was royal privileges, favours at court, tax exemption on imports and exports, the right to search any other ships without notice, and the right to keep any salvage they found. And they could do as they liked at sea – some might say this was nothing but a licence to pirate.

### Other eccentricities

#### DUNGENESS

Okay, I confess, Dungeness is in Kent, not Sussex *(see p.40)* but it is so eccentrically desolate and surreal that it's worth crossing borders for. Smoking power stations, bizarre ramshackle black-tarred houses dotted across the shingle, upturned wooden boats, miniature steam trains puffing across the landscape, two lighthouses, Derek Jarman's poignant garden, a great café – Dungeness is a world apart and in a league of its own.

---

**Getting there**                     National grid ref. TQ904173
❯ Car: off the A259 between Hastings and Rye.
❯ Train: National rail services from London/Victoria and Hastings.
❯ Bus: regular services from Hastings and Rye.
❯ Useful website: **www.winchelsea.net**

# INDEX